Romantic
Piano Anthology 2

30 Original Works

Selected and edited by Nils Franke

ED 12913

ISMN M-2201-2529-4
ISBN 978-1-902455-93-8

www.schott-music.com

Mainz · London · Madrid · New York · Paris · Prague · Tokyo · Toronto
© 2008 SCHOTT MUSIC Ltd, London · Printed in Germany

Acknowledgements:
I am grateful to Ateş Orga and Sally Anne Goodworth for their contribution to this edition. Their musical suggestions and recommendations of specific repertoire and/or composers have been invaluable. I am also indebted to Professor Emeritus Werner F. Kümmel for solving the riddle of translating a performance direction by Sergey Bortkiewicz.

Je voudrais remercier Ateş Orga et Sally Anne Goodworth pour leur contribution à la présente édition. Leurs suggestions musicales et leurs conseils avisés à propos de certains types de répertoire ou de compositeurs sont d'une valeur inestimable. Je dois également beaucoup au professeur émérite Werner F. Kümmel d'avoir résolu l'énigme posée par la traduction de certaines indications dans les partitions de Sergeï Bortkiewicz.

Ihre musikalischen Vorschläge und Empfehlungen spezieller Repertoirestücke und/oder Komponisten waren außerordentlich wertvoll. Außerdem bin ich Professor em. F. Kümmel zu Dank verpflichtet, der eine Spielanweisung von Sergey Bortkiewicz entschlüsselte.

ED 12913
British Library Cataloguing-in-Publication Data.
A catalogue record for this book is available from the British Library
ISMN M-2201-2529-4
ISBN 978-1-902455-93-8

© 2008 Schott Music Ltd, London

CD recorded in Champs Hill, West Sussex, 30th October 2007, on a Steinway D Concert Grand with Nils Franke, Piano
Producer: Ateş Orga
Editor: Ken Blair

French translation: Michaëla Rubi
German translation: Heike Brühl
Music setting by Woodrow
Typesetting by www.adamhaystudio.com
Printed in Germany S&Co.8177

Contents / Sommaire / Inhalt

The Pieces / Les pièces / Die Stücke

Introduction

The present collection of *Romantic Piano Anthologies* Volumes 1–4 (ED 12912 to ED 12915) is the result of teaching pupils of all ages and abilities. Whilst anthologies are, inevitably, a personal selection of repertoire, it has been my intention to include music that is idiomatically written and pianistically useful.

Stylistically, I have attempted to present a broad range of compositional styles of the romantic period from Schubert in the 1810s to Bortkiewicz in the 1920s. The selection of repertoire carefully balances the music of composers from different nationalities. It also provides a mixture of established teaching repertoire, lesser known works and the occasional rarity. However, the single most important aspect for selection has been the musical and technical value of a piece to potential students. The collection is intended to be both of pedagogical value to students and teachers, as well as indicative of the breadth and variety of romantic repertoire available.

Each anthology also contains a few pieces that are deliberate (yet manageable) challenges to the piano student, either in terms of musical complexity or technical requirements. Pieces 11, 13 and 24 may fall within that category. The repertoire is presented broadly in an order of ascending difficulty though I hope that teachers will feel able to treat the suggested sequence purely as a recommendation, rather than a restriction. Pieces included in this book are aimed at pianists of Grade 3 to 4 standard (UK) or intermediate players (USA) of some four to five years' playing experience (Europe).

The teaching notes are designed to help students by offering some suggestions on how to approach a particular piece. The commentary cannot, and is not intended to, replace the collaborative spirit of exploration that students and teachers share in a lesson.

The repertoire in this anthology should provide students with the intrinsic motivation to practice and thus enable them to enjoy the process of music making through study and performance.

Nils Franke

Introduction

Les quatre volumes de cette *Anthologie du piano romantique* (ED 12912 à ED 12915) sont l'aboutissement de mon expérience d'enseignant auprès d'élèves de tous âges au talent variable. Une anthologie reflète inévitablement les choix personnels de son auteur. Pour ma part, j'ai voulu rassembler ici un répertoire présentant à la fois une écriture idiomatique et une utilité du point de vue de l'apprentissage du piano.

Sur le plan stylistique, j'ai tenté de présenter un large éventail de styles issus de toute la période romantique, allant des années 1810 avec Schubert aux années 1920 avec Bortkiewicz. Cette sélection ménage également un juste équilibre entre les musiques de compositeurs de nationalités différentes. Enfin, des classiques éprouvés du répertoire pédagogique s'y trouvent mêlés à des œuvres moins connues, et même à quelques raretés. Cependant, le critère principal qui a présidé à mes choix est lié à la valeur musicale et technique de chaque pièce pour des élèves pianistes. Ces recueils, tels qu'ils sont conçus, présentent un intérêt pédagogique à la fois pour les élèves et pour leurs professeurs, tout en mettant en valeur la variété et l'étendue du répertoire romantique à notre disposition.

Chaque volume contient quelques pièces délibérément plus difficiles (cependant toujours surmontables) pour les élèves pianistes, que ce soit en termes de complexité musicale ou d'exigences tech-niques. Les pièces N° 11, 13 et 24 peuvent appartenir à cette catégorie. Le répertoire est présenté généralement dans un ordre croissant de difficulté, cependant j'espère que les professeurs de piano se sentiront libres de traiter la progression proposée comme une recommandation, sans restriction. Les pièces présentées dans le présent volume sont destinées à des pianistes de niveau 3 à 4 (Royaume-Uni), ou intermédiaire (USA) possédant quatre à cinq ans de pratique (Europe).

Les notes pédagogiques sont destinées à aider les élèves en leur proposant des suggestions quant à la façon d'aborder chaque pièce. Ce commentaire ne peut ni ne prétend remplacer l'esprit de collaboration et d'exploration que partagent le professeur et l'élève au cours d'une leçon.

J'espère que le répertoire réuni dans ce volume apportera aux élèves pianistes la motivation intérieure nécessaire à leur travail et leur permettra de prendre plaisir au processus musical par l'étude et l'interprétation.

Einleitung

Die vorliegende Sammlung der Bände 1–4 der *Romantic Piano Anthology* (ED 12912 bis ED 12915) ist aus dem Unterricht für Schüler aller Altersgruppen und Lernstufen entstanden. Eine Anthologie stellt zwar unweigerlich eine subjektive Repertoire-auswahl dar, doch war mein Anliegen eine Auswahl von Musikstücken, die idiomatisch geschrieben und in Bezug auf klavierspielerische Aspekte nützlich sind.

Stilistisch habe ich versucht, ein breites Spektrum kompositorischer Stilrichtungen der Romantik zu repräsentieren – von Schubert im ersten Jahrzehnt des 19. Jahrhunderts bis zu Bortkiewicz in den 1920er-Jahren. Die Repertoireauswahl stellt ein ausgewogenes Verhältnis der Musik von Komponisten unterschiedlicher Nationalitäten dar. Zudem ist sie eine Mischung aus bewährtem Unterrichtsmaterial, weniger bekannten Werken sowie einigen Raritäten. Der wichtigste Aspekt für die Auswahl war jedoch immer die musikalische und technische Bedeutung eines Stücks für die Schüler. Die Zusammenstellung soll zum einen für Schüler und Lehrer pädagogisch wertvoll sein und zum anderen die Bandbreite und Vielfalt des verfügbaren Romantik-Repertoires repräsentieren.

Jede Anthologie enthält außerdem einige Stücke, die entweder wegen ihrer musikalischen Komplexität oder ihrer technischen Anforderungen bewusste (jedoch zu bewältigende) Heraus-forderungen für die Klavierschüler sind. Die Stücke 11, 13 und 24 gehören zu dieser Kategorie. Das Repertoire ist größtenteils nach aufsteigendem Schwierigkeitsgrad geordnet, wobei ich hoffe, dass die Lehrer diese Reihenfolge lediglich als Empfehlung und nicht als Einschränkung auffassen. Die Stücke in diesem Buch richten sich an Pianisten der Stufe 3–4 (Großbritannien), Spieler der Mittelstufe (USA) bzw. Spieler mit vier bis fünf Jahren Spielerfahrung (restliches Europa).

Die Spielhinweise sollen die Schüler mit Hilfe von Vorschlägen an das jeweilige Stück heranführen. Die Kommentare können und sollen jedoch nicht die gemeinsame Beschäftigung von Lehrern und Schülern mit dem Stück ersetzen.

Die Stücke in dieser Anthologie dienen den Schülern als Motivation zum Üben, damit sie durch das Erlernen und Spielen der Stücke Spaß am Musizieren entwickeln.

1. Pastorale

Johann Burgmüller
(1806–1874)

2. Walzer

Franz Schubert
(1797–1828)

3. Wilder Reiter (Wild Horseman)

Robert Schumann
(1810–1856)

from • de • aus: ED 9010

4.

Enrique Granados
(1867–1916)

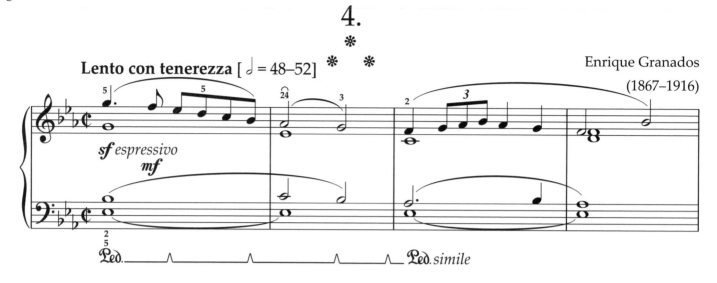

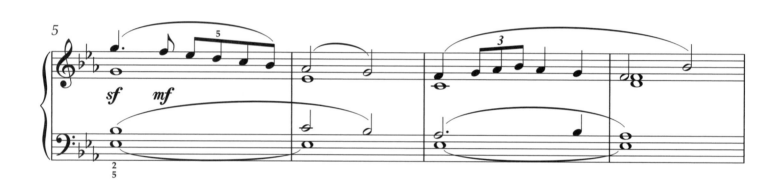

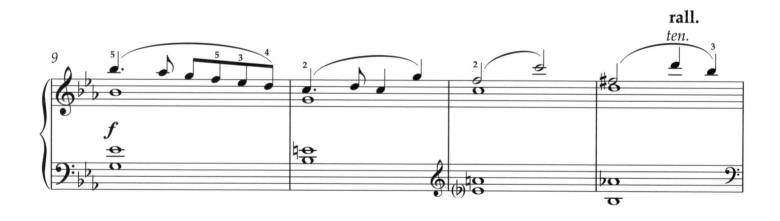

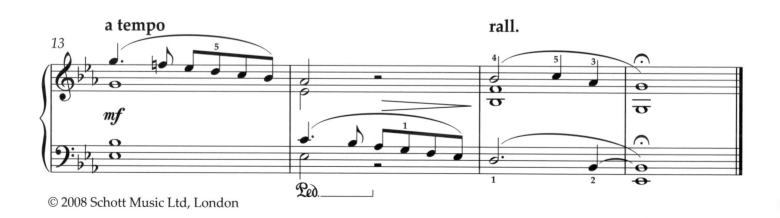

5. A Christmas Carol from Anjou

César Franck
(1822–1890)

Quasi allegro [♪ = 120–126]

6. Venedig. Gondellied
(Venice: Song of the Gondolier)

Sergey Bortkiewicz
(1877–1952)

Venedig - From 'Der Kleine Wanderer, Op. 21'

*from afar • de loin • aus der Ferne

7. Album Leaf

Antonín Dvořák
(1841–1904)

Moderato [♩ = 112–116]

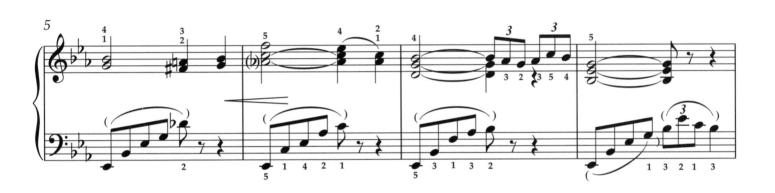

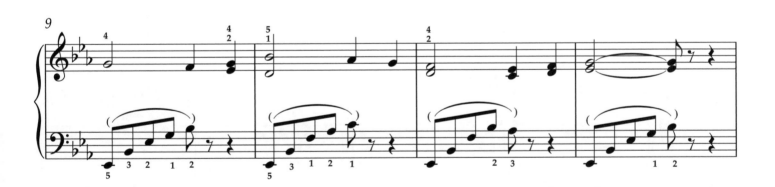

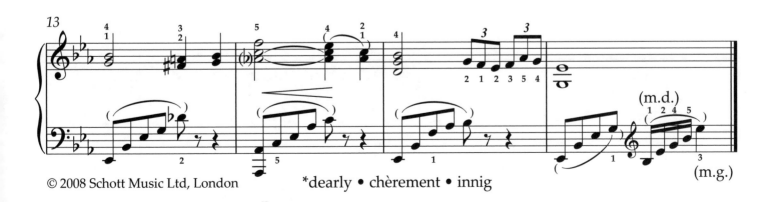

*dearly • chèrement • innig

8. Mazurka

Allegro moderato con molto delicatezza [♩ = 112–120]

Mikhail Glinka
(1804–1857)

9. Les plaintes d'une poupée
(A Doll's Lament)

César Franck
(1822–1890)

Andantino [♩ = 104–112]

10. Halling (Norwegian Dance)

Edvard Grieg
(1843–1907)

11. Capriccio

Zdenko Fibich
(1850–1900)

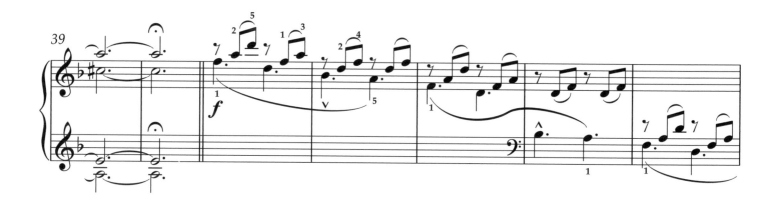

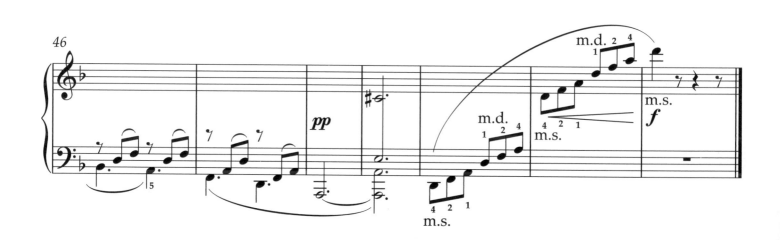

12. Musette

Charles Gounod
(1818–1893)

Impromptu

*slightly detached • légèrement détaché • leicht abgestoßen

13. Berceuse d'une poupée
(A Doll's Lullaby)

Sergey Lyapunov
(1859–1924)

14. Wiosna (Spring)

Frédéric Chopin
(1810–1849)

15. Old French Song

Peter Ilyich Tchaikovsky

(1840–1893)

Very moderate [♩ = 92–98]

p with feeling

16. Sizilianisch (Sicilienne)

Robert Schumann
(1810–1856)

from • de • aus: ED 9010

*mischievously • malicieusement

Da Capo al Fine
senza repetizione

17. Bådnlåt (Lullaby)

Edvard Grieg
(1843–1907)

18. Étude No. 22

Félix Le Couppey
(1811–1887)

19. Walzer

Franz Liszt
(1811–1886)

Fine

Da Capo al Fine

20. Dedicatoria (Dedication)

A mi hijo Eduardo*

Enrique Granados
(1867–1916)

*To my son Eduardo • À mon fils Eduardo • Für mein Sohn Eduardo

21. Der Engel (The Angel)

Andantino (♩ = 80–84)

Sergey Bortkiewicz
(1877–1952)

Der Engel - From 'Andersen's Märchen, Op. 30'

Chor der Engel*

*chorus of angels • choeur des anges

22. Piano Piece No. 4

Franz Liszt
(1811–1886)

Andantino [♩ = 92–98]

p *semplice (espressivo a piacere)*

un poco ritenuto

più ritenuto

smorz.

23. Walzer

Johannes Brahms

(1833–1897)

24. Gallop Marquis

Frédéric Chopin
(1810–1849)

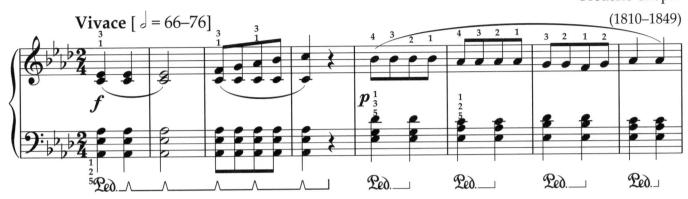

25. Ballade (Ballad)

Johann Burgmüller
(1806–1874)

Allegro con brio [♩. = 84–96]

26. Piece

Zdenko Fibich
(1850–1900)

27. Alvedans (Elves' Dance)

Molto allegro e sempre staccato [♩ = 148–156]

Edvard Grieg
(1843–1907)

28. Sweet Dream

Peter Tchaikovsky
(1840–1893)

Moderato [♩ = 98–104]

29. Bourée No. 2

Frédéric Chopin
(1810–1849)

Con ped.

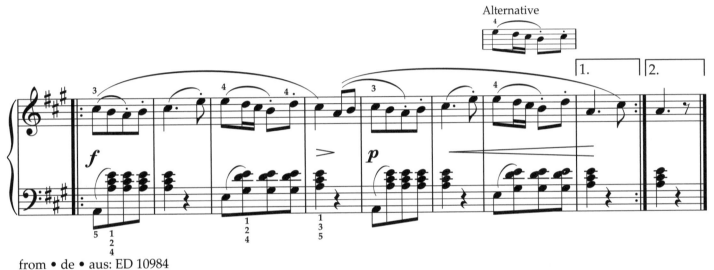

from • de • aus: ED 10984

30. Hungarian Dance

Hugo Reinhold
(1854–1935)

Printed in Germany • S&Co.8177

Teaching Notes

Sergey Bortkiewicz (1877–1952)

6. Venedig. Gondellied (Venice: Song of the Gondelier) Op. 21 No. 10

Bortkiewicz' performance indication of 'ondeggiando' means 'strolling' or 'walking casually' and is in some ways contradicted by the marking 'con moto'. The tempo to be chosen is therefore neither too slow nor too quick, however the performer can balance both! The longer phrases of bars 1–26 are a marked contrast to the shorter and more declamatory phrases in bars 26–42. One of the main challenges of the piece is the need to achieve an even left hand line in the first 26 bars of the piece, so that the shapes of the right hand melody line can be heard clearly. To achieve this, keep the fingers of the left hand very close to the keys. The fingering of 5/2 in bar 1 is the composer's own but you might want to try 5/1 or 4/1. The piece is taken from a collection of miniatures entitled '*The Little Wanderer*' in which the main character travels through a series of countries and cities. Volume 1 of the *Romantic Piano Anthologies* (ED 12912) contains the piece '*Through the Desert*' from the same collection.

21. Der Engel (The Angel) Op. 30 No. 4

This is a truly beautiful piece in its invention and harmonic simplicity. Creating a clear balance between the melody and accompaniment lines enables you to work on tone and touch control. Bars 80–99 sound almost Russian orthodox in their chorale texture and are somewhat reminiscent of Tchaikovsky's piece *At Church (Album for the Young, Op. 39)*. The piece comes from a collection of works based on Hans Christian Anderson's fairy tales.

Johannes Brahms (1833–1897)

23. Walzer Op. 39 No. 5

The waltz is taken from the composer's own arrangements of his 16 waltzes. In his transcription, Brahms expertly captures the essence of the pieces whilst simplifying some of the textures. In bars 1–8 bring out the rising top line whilst making the melodic lines in both hands equal in bars 9 and 11. Brahms wrote a number of transcriptions for a variety of purposes, including technical challenges (Weber's *Perpetuum mobile*; with the fast semiquaver work transferred to the left hand), birthday presents for friends (Variations from his own string sextet *Op. 18* arranged for solo piano), and study purposes (shorter Bach transcriptions).

Johann Burgmüller (1806–1874)

1. Pastorale Op. 100 No. 3

This short piece is an excellent study for the balancing of right hand melody notes against left hand chords. The chords, though securely placed, should always be subservient to the melody line. The use of the pedal is of course part of the style of this music though there are no pedal marks in the score. A discrete use of the pedal will enhance certain points of emphasis in the piece, such as the first beats in bars 11–14.

25. Ballade Op. 100 No. 15

This *Ballade* is, and always has been, a popular piece with both piano teachers and students. It lies well under the fingers, works at a number of different basic speeds, and is highly useful in the acquisition of coordination skills between right and left hand, particularly in bars 3–4. The middle section allows students to learn to place the melody notes on the first beat of the bar, whilst the left hand maintains the rhythmic framework. Bars 87–91 call for particularly good coordination. To develop this, practise these bars with your hands crossed, both right-over-left and left-over-right. Once you go back to playing this as written, you'll realize how useful crossed hand work can be!

Frédéric Chopin (1810–1849)

14. Wiosna (Spring) BI 117

This transcription, dated 5th February 1846, is one of two song arrangements that Chopin made of his own works; the other transcription is included in Volume 3 of the *Romantic Piano Anthologies* (ED 12914). The holding of a base note whilst the left hand plays another line is similar in principle to that of Tchaikovsky's *Old French Song* (No. 15 in this collection). To play both lines comfortably, you might find it useful to hold the low G whilst playing the upper line of the left hand as a slow detached quaver pattern. Once at ease, try both lines legato as written.

This rarely played miniature by Chopin was first published by Schott in 1968. The editor was Ateş Orga, who is also the producer of the CD of this album. Among pianists, *Wiosna* is best known in transcription by Franz Liszt, whose version is included in Volume 4 of the *Romantic Piano Anthologies* (ED 12915).

24. Gallop Marquis (KKp 1240a)

This is another rarely performed miniature by Chopin. The opening quaver motif is somewhat reminiscent of the composer's 'military' *Polonaise Op. 40 No. 1*. The main challenges of the piece are the jumps in the left hand in bars 13–19. To help the learning process, you might need to identify a manageable speed that is noticeably under tempo. Then play all single quaver notes in bars 13–19 one octave lower than written. Once comfortable, play the passage as written and gradually increase the tempo.

29. Boureé BI 160b No. 2

This piece was first published by Schott in 1968 alongside *Wiosna* (see above) and the *Boureé No. 1* (ED 12912). The editor of the edition, Ateş Orga, rightly suggests the replacing of the last quaver of bar 16 in the right hand with a C sharp for harmonic reasons.

Antonín Dvořák (1841–1904)

7. Album Leaf B158

The autograph of the piece is dated 21.7.1888. The composer does not give a dynamic indication at the beginning; instead the performance direction of 'dearly' reveals the mood of the piece and thus, rather indirectly, the dynamic level which is probably an upper 'piano'. The division of the arpeggio in the left hand of the last bar is an editorial suggestion only.

Zdenko Fibich (1850–1900)
11. Capriccio Op. deest
This short showpiece contains a couple of technical challenges. Firstly, the ascending scale patterns require hand crossings that are carefully prepared and therefore inaudible. Secondly, the repeated note patterns in bars 28 and 29 need detailed preparation; the given fingerings in this section are certainly tried and tested solutions. As so often in Fibich's music, the softer dynamics are the basis of his writing and the forte markings can be sharply articulated yet short–lived moments.

26. Piece Op. 47 No. 1
Dated 11.6.1895, this miniature is one of the *376 Moods, Impressions and Reminiscences* (1892–99), a cycle of piano pieces that developed as a result of the composer's infatuation with one of his students. The challenge in this piece is the sustaining of even repeated triplets within a limit range of dynamic shading. Inevitably, this will lead to experimentation with different qualities of sound and is as such an interesting alternative to Chopin's *Prelude Op. 28 No. 4*.

César Franck (1822–1890)
5. A Christmas Carol from Anjou (From: l'Organiste [1889–90])
There are two basic tempi in this piece. The opening speed is sustained until bar 16 after which it gradually gets slower until the new tempo is reached in bar 21. The minor/ major contrast of the two sections is therefore characterized both in terms of tonality and basic tempo. In bars 16–20 the part writing needs to be clearly audible, particularly in both treble and bass lines.

9. Les plaintes d'une poupée (A Doll's Lament, 1865)
The title of the piece might suggest a slower fundamental tempo but the choice of a major key makes this piece more likely to be reflective, rather than sad. The accompaniment line needs to be based on an evenly controlled legato sound that is subservient to the melody. Whilst the right hand carries the melody line for most of the piece, it is the left hand that needs to shine through in bars 37–44. The absence of phrase marks is an interesting feature of the piece. This creates the opportunity for student and teacher to experiment with the music and to personalize the score.

Mikhail Glinka (1804–1857)
8. Mazurka (1852)
Smaller hands may need to break the larger chords by turning them into arpeggio figurations. This applies particularly to the tenths in bars 4 and 7 and possibly to the octaves in bars 7 and 15. The *Mazurka* is a Polish country dance which is understood to have come from Mazovia, an area near Warsaw, Poland. It is a dance that is not necessarily fast but is characterized by an accent on the second beat of the bar,

a feature that Glinka incorporates throughout the piece (see bars 1 and 9, for an example). The *Mazurka* became a popular instrumental piece in the 19th century, particularly through Chopin's contribution to the genre.

Charles Gounod (1818–1893)
12. Musette (1863)
The *Musette* is a form of French bagpipe that contained 4 to 5 drones and was especially popular in the 17th and 18th centuries. Gounod imitates this drone in the 5ths of the left hand, over which an increasingly imaginative melody line unfolds. In bars 66 and 68ff. the first B of the ornament in the right hand should coincide with the chord of the left hand. Bars 49 to 56 offer a three part texture in which the dotted minims need to be given extra emphasis.

Enrique Granados (1867–1916)
4. *** Op. 1 No. 6
There is something Schumannesque about Granados' pieces *Op. 1*, both in spirit and occasionally in harmony. Following Schumann's example of publishing a piece whose title is deliberately not revealed (and marked with *** instead), Granados too provides a 'mystery' piece. Exquisite in its simplicity, the main challenge here is the production of a continuous legato line, aided by both finger and pedal legato.

20. Dedicatoria Op. 1 No. 1
Dedication is an excellent study in the variety of touch. As both accompaniment and bass line are potentially more resonant than the melody line of the 4th and 5th fingers, you might have to practice the piece initially with a 'forte' melody line to be able to contrast this with a 'piano' touch for the bass and accompaniment lines. Once comfortable, the dynamic levels can then be reduced proportionately. In bars 9 and 11 the melody line on the second beat of the bar appears off the beat. To emphasize this, play the top G slightly firmer than the preceding melody notes.

Edvard Grieg (1843–1907)
10. Halling Op. deest
The tempo for this Norwegian dance depends on the speed of the semiquavers in bar 17. Find a tempo at which you can comfortably play this section and then apply it to the opening of the piece. The acciaccaturas in bars 9 to 16 are best practised with a very light touch so that they don't interfere with the continuity of the melody line. Both the *Halling* and the subsequent *Lullaby* (see below) are taken from a collection of *6 Norwegian Melodies*, first published in 1886.

17. Bådnlåt (Lullaby) Op. deest
This *Lullaby* can be taken at a fairly slow speed but the composer's pedal markings may need to be modified to prevent the piece from sounding over-pedalled on the modern piano. Changing pedal every crotchet does give the piece sonority without it sounding overwhelming. To underline the hand crossing in bars 17 and 18 you might want to increase the dynamic level of the left hand notes above that of the right hand.

27. Alvedans (Elves' Dance) Op. 12 No. 4

The *Elves' Dance* is the fourth piece of Grieg's *Lyric Pieces Op. 12*. Written between 1864–7, it is technically and musically a very attractive piece to practise and perform. The right hand projects the melody until the upbeat to bar 7 where the left hand briefly takes over the melody line. The next challenge is the change of musical texture and register of the keyboard from bar 16 to 17. Here the start of bar 17 should be as much on time as the quick moving of the hands allows. Bars 23–30 require some careful rotation movement in the right hand to prevent muscular tension from arising and to emphasise the implied melodic line played by fingers 1–3. In the final three bars of the piece the composer marks staccato chords but the pedal to be held throughout. This can be understood as an instruction for greater sonority to which the staccato chords contribute. However, for the purpose of the recording I have chosen to amend the pedalling and to allow the staccato chords to be as short as possible.

Félix Le Couppey (1811–1887)

18. Étude Op. 22 No. 22

This piece is taken from the collection of *24 Études primarie*, first published by Schott. Two further etudes have already been included in Volume 1 of the *Romantic Piano Anthologies* (ED 12912). The metronome figure given is that of the composer. In terms of rhythm there could be the tendency to shorten the rest. It can therefore be useful to, at first, play the 6/8 pulse with a chord on every beat before practising the rhythm as notated.

Franz Liszt (1811–1886)

19. Walzer (1823)

This waltz sounds more Schubertian than Lisztian. Written in 1823, when the composer was only 12, it certainly contains none of the harmonic features that later works were to contain. Liszt's detailed articulation marks in bars 5 and 7, for example, highlight the dance characteristics of the piece and are therefore crucial to the understanding of the style and the finding of a tempo for this miniature. The waltz is a dance in 3/4 time that has possibly evolved from the somewhat slower Austrian *Ländler*.

22. Piano Piece No. 4 (1876)

This piece is a fine example of the composer's evolving style from the mid-1870s onwards. Taken from a set of 4 pieces that were written over a number of years, it is technically less involved writing than much of his earlier music. The style of the piece asks for pedalling throughout, although only bars 14–15 and 20–21 give specific information. A suitable alternative to Liszt's pedalling in bar 15 would be the very quick pedalling of each quaver which then contains a subtle overhang from the previous chord. This results in a slightly blurred sound which is still in line with the composer's original intention. The arpeggio of the last two bars should be spread out generously to allow time for the *più ritenuto* to continue to the end.

Sergey Lyapunov (1859–1924)

13. Berceuse d'une poupée (A Doll's Lullaby, 1914)

The rhythm of either hand is perfectly straight forward but combining both hands can result in some co-ordination problems. Working on bars 3–10 in units of 2½ bars at different speeds can help the process considerably (2 bars is the length of a phrase, plus allowing half a bar for the connection to the next phrase). Strangely, by the time there is an additional right hand part in bar 21 the co-ordination of both hands might get easier!

Hugo Reinhold (1854–1935)

30. Hungarian Dance Op. 19 No. 13

Reinhold's piece is an immediately memorable work that has the essential ingredients of some show pieces: it sounds more difficult than it is. Keep the rhythmic pattern absolutely strict except for the *ritardando* section in the middle of the piece. The trickiest bars are probably 5–8 and 26–29. Make sure that both hands are precisely together and fit the right hand to the left, not the other way round. That way it is easier to control and shape the togetherness of both hands.

Franz Schubert (1797–1828)

2. Walzer D365 No. 28

Schubert's *Waltz* is taken from a collection of waltzes written between 1816 and 21. In performance, this piece can be equally effective at different speeds and depending on whether or not one sees this as a waltz or being closer to a *Ländler*, the tempo might either be moderately lively or steady. In either case the main challenge is the even sound of the mordent. Practise the ornament as a triplet quaver figure that leads on to the next beat. This gives you time to aim for a clear and even sound.

Robert Schumann (1810–1856)

3. Wilder Reiter (Wild Horseman) Op. 68 No. 8

The *Wild Horseman* is equally effective in study and performance as it develops certain skills but also sounds like an effective and engaging recital piece. The technical advantage of the staccato quaver patterns is that they are written in two clearly identifiable hand positions per key. The slurred legato notes are a useful point of rest before moving on to the next set of staccato notes. However, in the end it is the quality of melodic invention that makes this piece a favourite with both piano teachers and students.

16. Sizilianisch Op. 68 No. 11

There is something both playful and slightly teasing about this piece. In the 6/8 section the two contrasting characters are clearly identifiable by the changes between '*p*' and '*f*' dynamics. Yet when learning the piece it is the 2/4 section that might require more time, in particular the left hand in bars 28 and 29. To position the 5th finger on F sharp, you might have to move the 3rd finger further down the 'a' than you are used to. Nevertheless, this is probably the most comfortable way of doing this.

Peter Ilyich Tchaikovsky (1840–1893)

15. Old French Song Op. 39 No. 16

A beautiful piece in the quality of melodic invention, the *Old French Song* is also a useful tool in the development of increased finger independence within the left hand. From a musical point of view, choose a speed that enables you to imagine a stringed instrument playing and connecting all melody notes. In bars 18–20 make the notes in the left hand as detached as possible without interfering with the continuity and dominance of the melody line in the right hand. Again, the score does not contain pedal marks but the use of the pedals is an integral part of the style.

28. Sweet Dream Op. 39 No. 21

Pedalling in this piece follows the melody line and with it the basic harmonic progression of the music. The dynamic contrasts are important, particularly the '*f*' sounds which, particularly at first playing, may seem a little harsh. Yet the lyrical qualities of the piece can only be fully appreciated when the dynamic contrast is in place. At specific cadence points, such as bars 8–9, 16–17 etc. it is only natural to take a little bit of time before returning to the overall tempo. In bars 21–24 and 29–32 keep the off–beat chords light so that the melodic flow of the crotchets is not interrupted.

Nils Franke

Biographical Notes

Sergey Bortkiewicz (1877–1952)

Ukrainian born Sergey Bortkiewicz spent the majority of his life working as a pianist and piano teacher in Austria and Germany. He studied composition with Lyadov at the St. Petersburg Conservatoire (1896–99) before continuing his studies in piano and composition with Reisenauer and Jadassohn at the Leipzig Conservatoire. Musically, Bortkiewicz' style is influenced by Chopin, Liszt and early Rachmaninov. Throughout his life, he remained faithful to a tonal form of composition, firmly rooted in the Russia of the late 19th century.

Johannes Brahms (1833–1897)

Though born in Hamburg, Brahms spent the majority of his life in Vienna where, from 1862 onwards, he became one of the 19th century's most influential composers. Brahms first came to prominence in 1853 when Robert Schumann enthusiastically reviewed his music, describing him as a 'genius'. Brahms developed a pianistic style of writing for the piano which is highly personal in texture, favouring chordal writing, double notes and polyrhythms. His compositional influence can be felt throughout the second half of the 19th and in the early part of the 20th centuries in several composers, including Reger and Stanford.

Johann Burgmüller (1806–1874)

Was born in Regensburg, Germany, and moved to Paris in 1832, where he worked as a sought-after piano teacher and composer of educational music. His Etudes *Opp. 73, 100* and *105* have long been an established part of the piano repertoire for students. Burgmüller wrote in an accessible style that can be described as melodically memorable and pianistically idiomatic.

Frédéric Chopin (1810–1849)

Polish by birth, Chopin moved to France in 1831 where he worked as a composer and private piano teacher. An infrequent performer in public, Chopin's reputation was built on select concert appearances and the publication of his music. Whilst often using 'popular' mediums, including *waltzes, preludes and etudes*, his style was as distinctive as it was timeless. Chopin can be credited with the establishing of the *ballade* as an instrumental piano piece, popularizing the *mazurka* in the 19th century and developing the genre of the *nocturne* after John Field. His most significant contribution to the development of piano technique was the two sets of *Etudes Opp. 10* and *25*.

Antonín Dvořák (1841–1904)

Dvořák was one of the few major 19th century composers who were not first study pianists. He studied violin and subsequently became a professional viola player before pursuing a career as a composer. Dvořák's writing was influenced by traditional Czech folk music and his close contact and personal friendship with Brahms. As a composition teacher he guided the next generation of young Czech composers, including Suk and Novák.

Zdenko Fibich (1850–1900)
The Czech composer Zdenko Fibich studied at the Leipzig Conservatoire from 1865–67. His teachers included Moscheles (piano), Richter and Jadassohn (composition). Fibich lived briefly in Paris and Mannheim before settling in Prague; here he worked as a theatre conductor and composer. His diverse output includes symphonies, songs, chamber music, opera and a collection of piano pieces entitled *376 Moods, Impressions and Reminiscences* (from which the two pieces in this anthology are taken). Many of these miniatures display his liking of very quiet dynamics and pensive moods.

César Franck (1822–1890)
César Franck had a distinguished musical career as a performer long before writing those works that secured his position as one of the great composers of his time. Born in Belgium in 1822, he went to Paris aged 13 to study composition at the Conservatoire. Completing his studies in 1842, he subsequently became a choirmaster and organist. Franck was well–known for his ability to improvise and continued to compose although it was only the music he wrote from the late 1870s onwards that brought him lasting international recognition as a composer.

Mikhail Glinka (1804–1857)
Mikhail Glinka has often been called the 'father of Russian music'. He was arguably the first Russian composer whose works were recognised outside Russia itself. Glinka spent time in Milan, Vienna and Berlin before returning to Russia. His subsequent opera *A life for the Tsar* (1836) established him as the leading Russian composer of his time. Glinka's music influenced a substantial number of younger Russian composers, most notably Balakirev, Rimsky-Korsakov and Mussorgsky.

Charles Gounod (1818–1893)
French composer, organist and conductor. Among his works are operas, some instrumental music, cantatas and church music. Gounod only wrote a small number of piano pieces, all of which display some of the characteristics of his style in terms of melodic and harmonic writing. His first major success was perhaps also his biggest and most enduring, that of the opera *Faust*, written in 1859.

Enrique Granados (1867–1916)
The Spanish composer and pianist Enrique Granados achieved the effortless fusion of an accessible piano style with musical material that is distinctly Spanish. A dedicated teacher, he founded his own music school, the Academia Granados which continued to exist after the composer's death under the leadership of his former pupil Frank Marshall. Granados wrote a substantial number of works for piano, ranging from finger exercises, studies and short character pieces to concert repertoire.

Edvard Grieg (1843–1907)
Norwegian composer, teacher and pianist. After initial training in his homeland, Grieg studied at the Leipzig Conservatoire. His music soon attracted the attention of his contemporaries; most notably Liszt, who in 1870 is said to have sight-read Grieg's piano concerto and offered its composer much encouragement. As a composer, Grieg is understood to have felt more comfortable writing shorter pieces. His most well-known creation for piano, a collection of 10 books of *Lyric Pieces* has always maintained a prominent position in the pianist's repertoire.

Félix Le Couppey (1811–1887)
Le Couppey was a Professor of Piano at the Paris Conservatoire, initially succeeding his own teacher as Professor of Harmony in 1843. In 1847 he deputised for the virtuoso pianist Henri Herz and was given his own piano class soon afterwards. Nowadays Le Couppey is best remembered for his influential pedagogical works which include *L'ABC du Piano* and *24 Études primaries*. He wrote a substantial number of works for beginners, most of which display his gift for melody. The present piece is taken from the collection of *24 Études primaries*, first published by Schott.

Franz Liszt (1811–1886)
Liszt was one of the most influential, controversial and colourful pianist-composers of the 19th century. A student of Beethoven's pupil Czerny, Liszt was a prodigy who, at the age of 17, was among the leading pianists of his day. Upon hearing Paganini in Paris in the early 1830s, Liszt decided to put himself through self-imposed further study to reach the level of proficiency as a pianist that would equal Paganini's command of the violin. Consequently, some of Liszt's music became extremely complex, earning him the reputation as an astonishing virtuoso. In 1848 Liszt withdrew from touring as a pianist to concentrate on conducting and composition. He championed many young composers, taught a new generation of virtuoso pianists and expanded the boundaries of harmony and tonality through his compositions.

Sergey Lyapunov (1859–1924)
Sergey Lyapunov was a Russian composer, pianist and conductor. His development as a composer was influenced by the Russian nationalism of Balakirev, eastern folk material and the pianism of Liszt. These characteristics fused to form a highly personal and distinctive style that favours elaborate and virtuosic writing. The piece included here is taken from a collection of *6 Easy Pieces*, written in 1914.

Hugo Reinhold (1854–1935)
Hugo Reinhold, born in Vienna, was a member of the choir at the Court Chappell until 1874. He subsequently studied composition with Bruckner at the Vienna Conservatoire, joining its staff in 1897. From 1909–25, Reinhold taught at the Academy of Music and Expressive Arts in Vienna. His music contains several collections for piano students, includ-

ing the *Jugendalbum Op. 27*, *Kleine melodische Etüden Op. 56 and Jugenderinnerungen Op. 5*. Most of these works demonstrate an easily accessible and tuneful way of writing.

Franz Schubert (1797–1828)

Unlike many of his contemporaries, Schubert was neither a virtuoso performer nor widely known as a composer during his lifetime. Originally setting out to become a primary school teacher, Schubert devoted himself full time to composition in 1817. He produced an astonishing output of works, both in quantity and quality, including over 600 songs, chamber music, 9 symphonies and many works for piano. Much of this music was not performed and certainly not published until after the composer's death. Schubert's style displays an ease of melodic invention that arguably has not been rivalled since.

Robert Schumann (1810–1856)

Robert Schumann was one of the 19th century's most influential composers. He developed a musical language all his own, shaped by two imaginary and contrasting characters: Florestan and Eusebius, representing the flamboyant and the expressive nature of his music (and of himself). Schumann drew on many literary inspirations, most notably the novels of E.T.A. Hoffmann, often creating music that is a direct representation of a literary source. Until 1839, Schumann wrote almost exclusively piano music, before branching out into chamber music, songs and orchestral works. His stylistic influence can be felt in a number of 19th century composers, from Kirchner to Tchaikovsky.

Peter Ilyich Tchaikovsky (1840–1893)

The Russian composer and conductor Peter Ilyich Tchaikovsky initially studied law and worked as a civil servant before turning to composition full time. Tchaikovsky found international recognition in the 1880s and 1890s. Much of his orchestral and ballet music is characterized by the quality of melodic invention and his rich orchestration. Tchaikovsky's piano writing ranges from the large-scale concert repertoire, such as the *Sonata Op. 37* to the *Children's Album Op. 39*, written for young players.

Nils Franke

Bibliography:

Hinson, Maurice,
Guide to the Pianist's Repertoire,
Bloomington and Indianapolis,
Indiana University Press, 2000

Prosnitz, Adolf,
Handbuch der Klavierliteratur,
Wien, Doblinger, 1908.

Rudthardt, Adolf,
Wegweiser durch die Klavierliteratur,
Leipzig and Zürich,
Gebrüder Hug & Co., 1910

Sadie, Stanley (ed.),
Grove Concise Dictionary of Music,
London, Macmillan Publishers, 1988

Sadie, Stanley (ed.),
Grove Dictionary of Music online,
accessed 13–15/02/2008

Notes pédagogiques

Sergeï Bortkiewicz (1877–1952)

6. Venedig. Gondellied (Venise : chanson du gondolier), Op. 21 N° 10

Les deux indications données par Bortkiewicz, d'une part *ondeggiando*, qui signifie « en flânant », ou « en marchant nonchalamment », et *con moto*, sont quelque peu contradictoires. Le tempo ne sera donc ni trop rapide ni trop lent, l'interprète pourra faire ses propres comparaisons ! Les phrases longues des mesures 1 à 26 présentent un contraste marqué par rapport aux phrases plus courtes et plus déclamatoires des mesures 26 à 42. L'une des difficultés principales de cette pièce réside dans la nécessité d'exécuter la main gauche avec beaucoup de régularité dans les 26 premières mesures, afin que les contours de la mélodie puissent ressortir clairement à la main droite. Pour y parvenir, gardez autant que possible les doigts de la main gauche très proches des touches. Le doigté 5/2 de la première mesure est celui proposé par le compositeur, mais vous aurez peut-être envie d'essayer 5/1 ou 4/1. Cette pièce est tirée d'un recueil de miniatures intitulé *The Little Wanderer* dans lequel le personnage principal voyage à travers toute une série de villes et de pays différents. *Through the Desert*, pièce tirée du même recueil, figure dans le volume 1 de cette anthologie (ED 12912).

21. Der Engel (L'ange), Op. 30 N° 4

Il s'agit d'une très jolie pièce de par son esprit d'invention et sa simplicité harmonique. Créer un équilibre clair entre la mélodie et l'accompagnement vous permettra de travailler sur le contrôle du son et du toucher. Les mesures 80 à 99, dans leur texture chorale, sonnent presque comme de la musique russe orthodoxe et évoquent quelque peu *At Church* (*Album pour la jeunesse, Op. 39*) de Tchaïkovski. Cette pièce est tirée d'un recueil d'œuvres inspirées par les contes de Hans Christian Andersen.

Johannes Brahms (1833–1897)

23. Valse, Op. 39 N° 5

Cette valse est tirée des arrangements de ses 16 valses que le compositeur a réalisés lui-même. Dans sa transcription, Brahms en capture l'essence avec talent tout en simplifiant légèrement leur texture. Dans les mesures 1 à 8, faites ressortir la ligne supérieure ascendante tandis que, dans les mesures 9 et 11, vous maintiendrez un équilibre entre les deux mains. Brahms a écrit de nombreuses transcriptions dans des objectifs divers, notamment pour lancer des défis techniques (le *Perpetuum mobile* de Weber, avec les passages rapides en doubles-croches transférés à la main gauche), pour faire des cadeaux d'anniversaire à ses amis (Variations sur son propre sextuor à cordes op.18 arrangé pour piano seul), ou simplement pour l'étude (transcriptions plus courtes d'œuvres de Bach).

Johann Burgmüller (1806–1874)

1. Pastorale Op. 100 N° 3

Cette courte pièce constitue une excellente étude pour s'entraîner à équilibrer la mélodie confiée à la main droite et les accords de la main gauche. Bien que placés avec assurance, ces accords devront toujours être subordonnés à la mélodie. L'utilisation de la pédale fait évidemment partie intégrante de cette musique, même s'il ne figure aucune indication de pédale dans la partition. Un usage discret de la pédale rehaussera certains moments d'intensité de la pièce, notamment les premiers temps des mesures 11 à 14.

25. Ballade Op. 100 N° 15

Cette *Ballade* jouit depuis toujours d'une grande popularité, aussi bien auprès des professeurs que de leurs élèves. Elle vient facilement sous les doigts, fonctionne à de nombreux tempos différents et s'avère très utile pour l'acquisition de la coordination entre les deux mains, notamment dans les mesures 3 et 4. La section centrale permet aux élèves d'apprendre à placer les notes de la mélodie sur le premier temps de la mesure tandis que la main gauche maintient la structure rythmique. Les mesures 87 à 91 nécessitent une coordination particulièrement accomplie. Pour la développer, exercez-vous à jouer ces mesures mains croisées, en alternant main droite au-dessus de la gauche puis main gauche au-dessus de la droite. Lorsque vous rejouerez ce passage tel qu'il est écrit, vous réaliserez à quel point ce travail mains croisées peut s'avérer utile !

Frédéric Chopin (1810–1849)

14. Wiosna (Printemps) BI 117

Datée du 5 février 1846, cette transcription est l'un des deux arrangements de chants que Chopin réalisa à partir de ses propres œuvres. L'autre transcription est incluse dans le volume 3 de la présente *Anthologie du piano romantique* (ED 12914). La tenue d'une note de base en même temps qu'une autre ligne mélodique à la main gauche relève d'un principe similaire à celui de la *Vieille chanson française de* Tchaïkovski (N° 15 de ce recueil). Pour jouer confortablement les deux voix, vous trouverez peut-être utile de tenir le *sol* grave tout en jouant la partie supérieure de la main gauche sur un motif de croches lentes et détachées. Lorsque vous serez à l'aise, essayez de jouer les deux lignes *legato*, comme elles sont écrites.

Rarement interprétée, cette miniature de Chopin a été publiée pour la première fois chez Schott en 1968. Elle avait été éditée par Ateş Orga qui est également le producteur du CD accompagnant ce volume. Les pianistes connaissent mieux la transcription de *Wiosna* réalisée par Franz Liszt qui figure dans le volume 4 de la présente *Anthologie du piano romantique* (ED 12915).

24. Gallop Marquis (KKp 1240a)

Voici une autre miniature rarement jouée de Chopin. Les croches du motif d'ouverture évoquent quelque peu la *Polonaise* « militaire » *Op. 40 N° 1* du compositeur. La plus grande difficulté de cette pièce réside dans les sauts de la main gauche aux mesures 13 à 19. Afin de faciliter le processus d'apprentissage, il vous sera peut-être nécessaire d'adopter une vitesse sensiblement inférieure au tempo demandé pour parvenir à les réaliser. Dans ce cas, jouez toutes les croches isolées des mesures 13 à 19 une octave plus bas que notées. Une fois que vous serez à l'aise, jouez ce passage tel qu'il est écrit et accélérez progressivement le tempo.

29. Bourrée BI 160b N° 2

Cette pièce a été publiée tout d'abord chez Schott en 1968 en même temps que *Wiosna* (voir ci-dessus) et la *Bourrée N° 1* (ED 12912). Pour des raisons harmoniques, Ateş Orga, responsable de cette première édition, suggère avec justesse de remplacer les dernières croches de la mesure 16 à la main droite par un *do* dièse.

Antonín Dvořák (1841–1904)

7. Album Leaf B158

Le manuscrit autographe de cette pièce est daté du 21.7.1888. Le compositeur ne donne aucune indication de dynamique au début. Cependant, la notation « tendrement » annonce l'atmosphère générale de la pièce et, de manière indirecte, le niveau de dynamique adapté, qui se situe probablement légèrement au dessus d'un *piano*. La division de l'arpège de la main gauche dans la dernière mesure n'est qu'une suggestion de l'éditeur.

Zdenko Fibich (1850–1900)

11. Capriccio

Cette pièce courte et brillante recèle quelques difficultés techniques. Tout d'abord, les motifs de gammes ascendantes requièrent des croisements de mains qui seront soigneusement préparés et donc indécelables à l'oreille. Ensuite, les motifs répétés des mesures 28 et 29 devront être également préparés avec soin. Les doigtés proposés pour ce passage sont des solutions testées et éprouvées. Comme c'est fréquemment le cas dans la musique de Fibich, les dynamiques douces sont à la base de son écriture et les passages *forte* peuvent être nettement accentués, même s'ils ne durent jamais très longtemps.

26. Pièce Op. 47 N° 1

Datée du 11.6.1895, cette miniature est l'une des *376 Atmosphères, Impressions et souvenirs* (1892-99), cycle de pièces pour piano composé à la suite d'une toquade du compositeur pour une de ses élèves. La difficulté de cette pièce réside dans la répétition régulière de triolets dans une variété limitée de nuances dynamiques. Cela conduira inévitablement à des expérimentations sur différentes qualités de timbre et constitue de ce fait une alternative intéressante au *Prélude* op. 28 N° 4 de Chopin.

César Franck (1822–1890)

5. Noël angevin (tiré de : L'organiste [1889-90])

Cette pièce présente deux tempos principaux. Le tempo d'ouverture est maintenu jusqu'à la mesure 16 et ralentit ensuite progressivement jusqu'à obtention du nouveau tempo à la mesure 21. Le contraste majeur/mineur des deux parties se trouve ainsi défini à la fois en termes de tonalité et de tempo. Aux mesures 16 à 21, les différentes voix devront ressortir clairement, notamment la voix grave et la voix aiguë.

9. Les plaintes d'une poupée (1865)

Le titre de cette pièce suggère un tempo relativement lent, mais le choix d'une tonalité majeure lui confère un caractère moins triste que réfléchi. Les voix d'accompagnement devront reposer sur un *legato* égal et contrôlé toujours au service de la mélodie. Tandis que la main droite porte la mélodie pendant presque toute la pièce, c'est la main gauche qui devra briller entre les mesures 37 à 74. L'absence d'indications de phrasé est une des caractéristiques importantes de cette pièce et offre au professeur et à son élève la possibilité de faire toutes sortes d'expérimentations et de personnaliser la partition.

Mikhaïl Glinka (1804–1857)

8. Mazurka (1852)

Les petites mains seront peut-être contraintes de briser les grands accords en les arpégeant. Ce sera le cas notamment pour les écarts de dixièmes des mesures 4 et 7 et éventuellement pour les octaves des mesures 7 et 15. La *Mazurka* est une danse folklorique polonaise sans doute originaire de la région de Mazovia, non loin de Varsovie. Il s'agit d'une danse qui n'est pas obligatoirement rapide, mais qui est caractérisée par l'accent porté sur le second temps de la mesure, particularité que Glinka incorpore dans la pièce (voir mesures 1 et 9 par exemple). La Mazurka devint très populaire dans la musique instrumentale du 19e siècle, en particulier grâce aux contributions de Chopin à ce genre.

Charles Gounod (1818–1893)

12. Musette (1863)

La musette, de l'instrument du même nom, était une danse très populaire aux 17e et 18e siècles, caractérisée par la présence de 4 ou 5 bourdons. Gounod imite ce procédé à travers les quintes de la main gauche au dessus desquelles se développe une mélodie de plus en plus imaginative. Aux mesures 66 et 68 et suivantes, le premier *si*b de l'ornementation à la main droite devra coïncider avec l'accord de la main gauche. Les mesures 49 à 56 offrent une texture à trois voix dans laquelle les blanches pointées devront être particulièrement accentuées.

Enrique Granados (1867–1916)

4. *** Op. 1 N° 6

Il y a quelque chose de schumannien dans les pièces de l'opus 1 de Granados, à la fois dans l'esprit et (parfois) dans l'harmonie. À l'instar de Schumann, il publie une pièce dont le titre est volontairement tenu secret (et marqué de trois étoiles ***), nous proposant ainsi une pièce « mystère ». Raffinée dans sa simplicité, la difficulté principale sera ici de maintenir la continuité du *legato* à l'aide du mouvement des doigts et de la pédale.

20. Dedicatoria Op.1 N° 1

Il s'agit d'une étude excellente pour exercer la variété des touchers. Comme la basse et l'accompagnement sont tous deux potentiellement plus résonants que la ligne mélodique des 4ᵉ et 5ᵉ doigts, il vous sera peut-être nécessaire de travailler cette pièce en jouant cette ligne mélodique *forte* afin d'obtenir un contraste suffisant par rapport à la basse et à l'accompagnement que vous jouerez *piano*. Lorsque vous serez à l'aise, vous pourrez diminuer proportionnellement les effets dynamiques. Aux mesures 9 et 11, la ligne mélodique du second temps de la mesure apparaît donc sur le temps faible. Afin de l'accentuer, jouez le *sol* aigu un peu plus fermement que les notes précédentes de la mélodie.

Edvard Grieg (1843–1907)
10. Halling Op. deest

Le tempo de cette danse norvégienne dépend de la vitesse des doubles-croches de la mesure 17. Trouvez un tempo qui vous permettra de jouer ce passage confortablement et appliquez-le ensuite au début de la pièce. Les *acciaccatura* des mesures 9 à 16 seront interprétées avec beaucoup de légèreté afin de ne pas interférer dans la continuité de la ligne mélodique. *Halling* et la *Berceuse* (voir ci-dessous) sont deux pièces tirées du recueil des *Six Mélodies norvégiennes*, publié pour la première fois en 1886.

17. Bådnlåt (Berceuse) Op. deest

Cette berceuse peut être prise à un tempo relativement lent, mais les indications de pédale du compositeur devront peut-être alors être modifiées afin d'éviter une sonorité noyée par la pédale sur des pianos modernes. Un changement de pédale à chaque noire donne à cette pièce toute sa sonorité sans que l'effet devienne envahissant. Afin de souligner le croisement de mains des mesures 17 et 18, vous voudrez peut-être augmenter la dynamique des notes de la main gauche au dessus de celle de la main droite.

27. Alvedans (Danse des elfes) Op. 12 N° 4

La danse des elfes est le quatrième morceau des *Pièces lyriques* op. 12 de Grieg. Écrit entre 1864 et 1867, c'est un morceau très agréable à travailler et à jouer, tant du point de vue technique que musical. La main droite projette la mélodie jusqu'à la levée de la mesure 7 où c'est au tour de la main gauche de reprendre brièvement la ligne mélodique. La difficulté suivante réside dans le changement de texture musicale et de registre sur le clavier intervenant aux mesures 16 et 17. Le début de la mesure 17 devra être aussi bien en place que le permet le rapide mouvement des mains. Dans les mesures 23 à 30, la main droite effectuera avec précaution un mouvement de rotation afin de prévenir les tensions musculaires et d'accentuer la ligne mélodique au 1ᵉʳ et 3ᵉ doigt. Dans les trois dernières mesures, les accords ont été notés *staccato* par le compositeur, alors que la pédale doit être maintenue en même temps. Cela peut être interprété comme la demande d'une sonorité plus ample à laquelle contribuent les accords *staccato*. Cependant, pour les besoins de l'enregistrement, j'ai choisi de modifier le jeu de pédale et de permettre ainsi aux accords *staccato* d'être aussi brefs que possible.

Félix Le Couppey (1811–1887)
18. Étude Op. 22 N° 22

Cette pièce est tirée du recueil des *24 Études primaires*, publié pour la première fois chez Schott. Deux autres études de ce recueil ont déjà été incluses au premier volume de la présente *Anthologie du piano romantique* (ED 12912). Les données métronomiques sont celles du compositeur. En termes de rythme, vous serez peut être tenté de raccourcir les silences. C'est pourquoi il pourra vous être utile de jouer la mesure à 6/8 en plaçant un accord sur chaque pulsation avant de jouer le rythme tel qu'il est écrit.

Franz Liszt (1811–1886)
19. Valse (1823)

Cette valse semble plus schubertienne que lisztienne. Écrite en 1823, alors que le compositeur n'avait que 12 ans, elle ne présente aucune des caractéristiques harmoniques de ses œuvres plus tardives. Les indications d'articulation très détaillées données par Liszt aux mesures 5 et 7, par exemple, mettent en valeur le caractère dansant de la pièce et sont de ce fait cruciales pour la compréhension du style et la recherche d'un tempo adapté pour cette miniature. La valse est une danse à trois temps (3/4) dont on pense qu'elle est peut-être issue du *Ländler* autrichien plus lent.

22. Piano Piece N° 4 (1876)

Cette pièce est un parfait exemple de l'évolution du style du compositeur à partir du milieu des années 1870. Tirée d'un ensemble de quatre pièces écrites sur plusieurs années, l'écriture est moins investie techniquement que celle d'œuvres antérieures. Le style de cette pièce exige un jeu de pédales permanent, bien que cela ne soit indiqué explicitement qu'aux mesures 14 et 15 puis 20 et 21. Une alternative possible aux indications de pédale de Liszt de la mesure 15 serait d'enfoncer rapidement la pédale sur chaque croche, lui permettant de conserver ainsi une résonance subtile de l'accord précédant. Le léger effet de flou ainsi obtenu correspond tout à fait à l'intention du compositeur. L'arpège des deux dernières mesures devra être déployé généreusement afin de laisser le temps au *più ritenuto* de se poursuivre jusqu'à la fin.

Sergeï Lyapunov (1859–1924)
13. Berceuse d'une poupée (1914)

Le rythme de chaque main est relativement simple, mais la combinaison des deux peut provoquer quelques difficultés de coordination. Afin de faciliter avantageusement le processus d'apprentissage, vous pourrez travailler les mesures 3 à 10 par groupes de deux mesures et demie à différents tempos (les phrases font deux mesures, mais la demi-mesure complémentaire permet de faire la jonction avec la phrase suivante). Étrangement, au moment où apparaît une voix supplémentaire à la main droite, la coordination des deux mains semble plus facile !

Hugo Reinhold (1854–1935)

30. Danse hongroise Op. 19 N° 13

La pièce de Reinhold se grave immédiatement dans la mémoire, car elle possède tous les ingrédients de certaines pièces brillantes : elle paraît plus difficile qu'elle ne l'est en réalité. Veillez à respecter strictement le motif rythmique sauf dans le passage noté *ritardando* au milieu. Les mesures les plus difficiles sont sans doute les mesures 5 à 8 et les mesures 26 à 29. Assurez-vous que les deux mains sont parfaitement synchronisées ; calez la main droite sur la main gauche et non l'inverse. Il vous sera ainsi plus facile de maîtriser la coordination des deux mains.

Franz Schubert (1797–1828)

2. Valse D365 N° 2

Cette valse de Schubert est tirée d'un recueil de valses écrites entre 1816 et 1821. En concert, elle fera autant d'effet à différents tempos. Selon que vous l'envisagez plus comme une valse ou comme un *Ländler*, le tempo sera relativement animé ou plus stable. Dans un cas comme dans l'autre, la difficulté principale résidera dans la sonorité équilibrée du mordant. Exercez-vous à réaliser cet ornement comme un triolet de croches menant au temps suivant. Cela vous donnera le temps de rechercher une sonorité claire et équilibrée.

Robert Schumann (1810–1856)

3. Wilder Reiter (Le cavalier sauvage) Op. 68 N° 8

Le cavalier sauvage sera aussi efficace lorsque vous le travaillerez qu'en concert, car il développe certaines compétences, mais sonne aussi comme une véritable et très agréable pièce de récital. L'avantage technique des motifs de croches *staccato* est qu'ils sont écrits dans deux positions des mains clairement identifiables par tonalité. Les notes liées du *legato* ménagent un temps de repos utile avant de poursuivre avec les notes *staccato* suivantes. Cependant, c'est surtout la qualité de l'invention mélodique qui fait de cette pièce un favori à la fois des professeurs et des élèves.

16. Sizilianisch Op. 68 N° 11

Cette pièce possède un caractère à la fois ludique et légèrement espiègle. Le passage en 6/8 permet d'identifier clairement deux personnages grâce à l'alternance entre les dynamiques *p* et *f*. Cependant, lorsque vous apprendrez à la jouer, le passage en 2/4 vous demandera peut-être plus de temps, en particulier la main gauche aux mesures 28 et 29. Afin de positionner le 5ᵉ doigt sur le *fa* aigu vous devrez peut-être déplacer votre 3ᵉ doigt plus loin sur le *la* que vous n'en avez l'habitude. Quoiqu'il en soit, c'est sans doute la façon la plus confortable d'y parvenir.

Piotr Ilitch Tchaïkovski (1840–1893)

15. Vieille chanson française Op. 39 N° 16

Pièce magnifique de par la qualité de son invention mélodique, cette *Vieille chanson française* est également un outil très utile pour développer l'indépendance des doigts à la main gauche. D'un point de vue musical, choisissez un tempo qui vous permettra d'imaginer un instrument à cordes jouant toutes les notes de la mélodie en les reliant. Aux mesures 18 à 20, détachez autant que possible les notes de la main gauche sans interférer dans la continuité et la prépondérance de la ligne mélodique de la main droite. Cette fois encore, la partition ne contient aucune indication de pédale, mais l'utilisation de la pédale est partie intégrante de ce style de musique.

28. Sweet Dream Op. 39 N° 21

Le jeu de pédale suit ici la ligne mélodique ainsi que la progression harmonique générale. Les contrastes dynamiques sont importants, notamment les *f* qui, en particulier lorsque vous jouerez cette pièce pour la première fois, vous paraîtront un peu rudes. Cependant, les qualités lyriques de cette pièce ne pourront être pleinement appréciées que lorsque les contrastes dynamiques seront bien en place. Après certaines cadences, comme aux mesures 8-9, 16-17 etc., il est normal de prendre un peu de temps avant de revenir au tempo général. Aux mesures 21 à 24 et 29 à 32, jouez les accords à contretemps avec légèreté afin de ne pas interrompre le flux mélodique des noires.

Notes biographiques

Sergeï Bortkiewicz (1877–1952)
D'origine ukrainienne, Sergeï Bortkiewicz consacra la majeure partie de sa vie à l'enseignement et à son activité de concertiste en Autriche et en Allemagne. Il étudia la composition auprès de Lyadov au conservatoire de Saint-Pétersbourg (1896-1899) avant de poursuivre ses études de piano et de composition avec Reisenauer et Jadassohn au conservatoire de Leipzig. D'un point de vue musical, son style est influencé par Chopin, Liszt et les premières œuvres de Rachmaninov. Tout au long de sa vie, il restera fidèle à une forme tonale de composition, fermement enracinée dans la fin du 19e siècle.

Johannes Brahms (1833–1897)
Bien que natif de Hambourg, Brahms passa la plus grande partie de sa vie à Vienne ou il devint, à partir de 1862, l'un des compositeurs les plus influents du 19e siècle. Brahms sortit de l'ombre pour la première fois en 1853, lorsque Schumann écrivit des critiques enthousiastes sur sa musique, le décrivant comme un « génie ». Brahms a développé un style d'écriture pianistique très personnel de par sa texture favorisant l'écriture harmonique, les notes redoublées et la polyrythmie. Son influence en tant que compositeur se ressent dans toute la seconde moitié du 19e siècle et au début du 20e siècle auprès de nombreux compositeurs dont notamment Reger et Stanford.

Johann Burgmüller (1806–1874)
Né à Regensburg en Allemagne, il s'installa à Paris en 1832 où il fut un professeur de piano très recherché et composa de nombreuses pièces pédagogiques. Ses études Opp. 73, 100 et 105 ont longtemps fait partie du répertoire des apprentis pianistes. Burgmüller écrivait dans un style accessible qui peut être décrit comme facilement mémorisable mélodiquement et idiomatique du point de vue pianistique.

Frédéric Chopin (1810–1849)
Polonais de naissance, Chopin s'installa en France en 1831 ou il s'établit en tant que compositeur et professeur de piano en privé. Chopin se produisait rarement en public et sa réputation se fondait sur de rares apparitions en concert ainsi que sur la publication de sa musique. Tandis que les types de morceaux utilisés étaient souvent populaires, incluant valses, préludes et études, son style était tout à fait particulier et intemporel. Chopin peut être considéré comme celui qui a introduit la *ballade* dans la musique instrumentale pour piano, popularisé la *mazurka* au 19e siècle et développé le genre du *nocturne* à la suite de John Field. Ses deux recueils d'*Études* Opp. 10 et 25 sont sa contribution la plus significative au développement de la technique du piano.

Antonín Dvořák (1841–1904)
Dvořák était l'un des rares compositeurs importants du 19e siècle à ne pas être pianiste. Il étudia le violon et devint pro-fesseur d'alto professionnel avant d'embrasser la carrière de compositeur. Son écriture est influencée par la musique populaire tchèque et par son amitié personnelle avec Brahms. En tant que professeur de composition, il servit de guide à la génération suivante de jeunes compositeurs tchèques, dont Suk et Novák.

Zdenko Fibich (1850–1900)
Le compositeur tchèque Zdenko Fibich fit ses études musicales au conservatoire de Leipzig entre 1865 et 1867. Parmi ses professeurs, il y eut Moscheles (piano), Richter et Jadassohn (composition). Fibich séjourna quelques temps à Paris puis Mannheim avant de s'installer à Prague où il travailla en tant que directeur musical dans un théâtre et en tant que compositeur. Ses diverses productions comprennent des symphonies, de la musique vocale, de la musique de chambre, des opéras, ainsi qu'un recueil de pièces pour piano intitulé *376 Atmosphères, impressions et souvenirs* (nous en reprenons deux dans cette anthologie). Parmi ces miniatures, nombreuses sont celles qui reflètent sa prédilection pour les dynamiques calmes et les atmosphères pensives.

César Franck (1822–1890)
César Franck connut une belle carrière d'interprète bien longtemps avant d'écrire les œuvres qui le consacrèrent comme l'un des plus grands compositeurs de son temps. Né en Belgique en 1822, il vint à Paris à l'âge de 13 ans afin d'étudier la composition au conservatoire. En 1842, ses études terminées, il devint chef de chœur et organiste. Franck était réputé pour sa capacité d'improvisation et continua à composer, même si se sont les œuvres qu'il écrivit à partir de la fin des années 1870 qui lui apportèrent la véritable et durable reconnaissance internationale en tant que compositeur.

Mikhaïl Glinka (1804–1857)
Mikhaïl Glinka a souvent été désigné comme le « père de la musique russe ». On peut dire qu'il est le premier compositeur russe dont les œuvres ont été reconnues en dehors de la Russie elle-même. Glinka fit des séjours à Milan, Vienne et Berlin avant de retourner en Russie. Son opéra *La vie pour le tsar* (1836) fit de lui le compositeur russe le plus important de son temps. La musique de Glinka a influencé un grand nombre de jeunes compositeurs russes dont en particulier Balakirev, Rimski-Korsakov et Moussorgski.

Charles Gounod (1818–1893)
Compositeur, organiste et chef d'orchestre français. Ses œuvres comptent des opéras, de la musique instrumentale, des cantates et de la musique religieuse. Gounod n'a écrit que très peu d'œuvres pour piano. Toutes présentent certaines caractéristiques de son style en termes d'écriture harmonique et mélodique. Son premier succès important fut sans doute aussi le plus grand et le plus durable, il s'agit de son opéra, *Faust*, écrit en 1859.

Enrique Granados (1867–1916)
Le pianiste et compositeur espagnol Enrique Granados a

réussi à fusionner sans effort un style de piano accessible avec des matériaux musicaux typiquement espagnols. Prenant sont rôle de professeur de piano très au sérieux, il fonda sa propre école de musique, l'académie Granados, qui continua à exister après la mort du compositeur sous la conduite de son ancien élève, Frank Marshall. Granados a écrit un grand nombre de courtes pièces de caractère, d'études, ainsi que du répertoire de concert.

Edvard Grieg (1843–1907)

Professeur, compositeur et pianiste norvégien. Après une formation initiale dans son pays natal, Grieg étudia au conservatoire de Leipzig. Sa musique attira rapidement l'attention de ses contemporains et en particulier de Liszt dont on dit qu'en 1870 il déchiffra le concerto pour piano de Grieg et encouragea fortement le compositeur. En tant que compositeur, Grieg semble cependant avoir été plus à l'aise dans la composition de pièces plus courtes. Sa création pour piano la plus connue, une collection de 10 recueils de *Pièces lyriques*, a toujours gardé une position privilégiée dans le répertoire des pianistes.

Félix Le Couppey (1811–1887)

Le Couppey était professeur de piano au conservatoire de Paris, où il a commencé en 1843 par succéder à son propre professeur dans la classe d'harmonie. En 1847, il assura l'intérim du pianiste virtuose Henri Herz et obtint sa propre classe de piano peu après. Actuellement, Le Couppey est connu essentiellement pour ses pièces pédagogiques qui incluent *L'ABC du Piano* et les *24 Études primaires*. Il a écrit un grand nombre de pièces pour débutants, dont la plupart dénotent ses dons pour la mélodie. La pièce présentée ici est tirée des *24 Études primaires*, publiées initialement chez Schott.

Franz Liszt (1811–1886)

Liszt est l'un des compositeurs les plus influents, mais aussi les plus controversés et les plus originaux parmi les pianistes-compositeurs du 19e siècle. Élève de Czerny, lui-même élève de Beethoven, Liszt était un prodige qui à l'âge de 17 ans comptait déjà parmi les principaux pianistes de son temps. Après avoir entendu Paganini en concert à Paris au début des années 1830, il s'imposa un programme d'études complémentaires afin d'acquérir au piano un niveau d'excellence comparable à celui de Paganini au violon. De ce fait, certaines de ses compositions sont très complexes, lui valant la réputation d'un virtuose éblouissant. En 1848, il cessa ses tournées d'interprète pour se consacrer à la direction et à la composition. Il prit la défense de nombreux jeunes compositeurs et forma toute une nouvelle génération de pianistes virtuoses. Dans ses compositions, il s'ingénia à repousser les frontières de l'harmonie et de la tonalité.

Sergeï Lyapunov (1859–1924)

Sergeï Lyapunov était un compositeur, pianiste et chef d'orchestre russe. Son évolution en tant que compositeur fut influencée par le nationalisme de Balakirev, les matériaux populaires issus de l'Est et le pianisme lisztien. Ces caractéristiques fusionnèrent pour former un style très personnel et original favorisant une écriture élaborée et virtuose. La pièce présentée ici est tirée d'un recueil de *Six Pièces faciles*, écrites en 1914.

Hugo Reinhold (1854–1935)

Hugo Reinhold, natif de Vienne, fut membre du chœur de la Chapelle royale jusqu'en 1874. Il étudia ensuite la composition avec Bruckner au conservatoire de Vienne puis rejoignit l'équipe enseignante en 1897. De 1909 à 1925, il enseigna à l'académie de musique et d'arts dramatique de Vienne. Son œuvre comprend de nombreux recueils de musique pour piano dont *Jugendalbum Op. 27*, *Kleine melodische Etüden Op. 56* et *Jugenderinnerungen Op. 5*. La plupart de ses œuvres dénotent une écriture facilement accessible et très mélodieuse.

Franz Schubert (1797–1828)

Contrairement à nombre de ses contemporains, Schubert n'était ni un virtuose, ni très connu comme compositeur de son vivant. Destiné au départ à une carrière d'enseignant en école primaire, Schubert ne se consacra entièrement à la composition qu'à partir de 1817. Sa production est étonnamment abondante, à la fois en qualité et en quantité, et comprend plus de six cents lieder, de la musique de chambre, neuf symphonies et de nombreuses œuvres pour piano. Nombre de ces œuvres n'ont été ni jouées ni éditées de son vivant. Le style de Schubert dénote une aisance dans l'invention mélodique qui n'a sans doute jamais été égalée depuis.

Robert Schumann (1810–1856)

Robert Schumann était l'un des plus grands compositeurs du 19e siècle. Il a développé un langage musical personnel façonné par deux personnages contrastés : Florestan et Eusebius, qui représentent la nature expressive et flamboyante de sa musique (et de lui-même). Schumann puisait son inspiration dans de nombreuses sources littéraires, en particulier les nouvelles de E.T.A. Hoffmann, concevant des musiques illustrant directement la source littéraire considérée. Jusqu'en 1839, Schumann écrivit presque exclusivement de la musique pour piano, des lieder et des œuvres pour orchestre. Son influence stylistique a touché de nombreux compositeurs du 19e siècle, de Kirchner à Tchaïkovski.

Piotr Ilitch Tchaïkovski (1840–1893)

Le compositeur et chef d'orchestre russe Piotr Ilitch Tchaïkovski commença par faire des études de droit et par occuper un emploi de fonctionnaire avant de se consacrer à plein temps à la composition. Tchaïkovski obtint la reconnaissance internationale entre les années 1880 et 1890. La plupart de ses œuvres pour orchestre et de ses ballets se caractérisent par la qualité de l'invention mélodique et par la richesse de l'orchestration. Les œuvres pour piano de Tchaïkovski vont du répertoire de concert de grande envergure, comme la *Sonate Op. 37*, à l'*Album pour les enfants*, écrit pour les jeunes pianistes.

Spielhinweise

Sergej Bortkiewicz (1877–1952)
6. Venedig. Gondellied (Venice: Song of the Gondelier) Op. 21 No. 10
Bortkiewicz' Spielanweisung ‚ondeggiando' bedeutet ‚schlendernd' bzw. ‚wogend' und steht in gewisser Hinsicht im Gegensatz zur Anweisung ‚con moto'. Das Tempo sollte daher weder zu langsam noch zu schnell sein; man kann natürlich auch beides spielen! Die längeren Phrasen in Takt 1-26 stellen einen deutlichen Kontrast zu den kürzeren, pathetischeren Phrasen in Takt 26-42 dar. Eine der größten Herausforderungen des Stücks ist, die ersten 26 Takte mit der linken Hand so gleichmäßig zu spielen, dass die Melodiefiguren in der rechten Hand deutlich zu hören sind. Zu diesem Zweck müssen die Finger der linken Hand dicht an den Tasten bleiben. Der Fingersatz 5/2 in Takt 1 stammt vom Komponisten; man kann jedoch auch 5/1 oder 4/1 ausprobieren. Das Stück stammt aus einer Sammlung von Miniaturen mit dem Titel ‚*Der kleine Wanderer*', in denen die Hauptfigur durch eine Reihe von Ländern und Städten wandert. Band 1 der *Romantic Piano Anthology* (ED 12912) enthält das Stück ‚*Through the Desert*' (‚*Durch die Wüste*') aus derselben Sammlung.

21. Der Engel (The Angel) Op. 30 No. 4
Ein herrliches Stück, das sich durch Einfallsreichtum und einfache Harmonien auszeichnet. Um eine gute Ausgewogenheit zwischen Melodie und Begleitung zu erzielen, sollte man am Klang und der Anschlagstechnik arbeiten. Die Takte 80-99 klingen mit ihrem choralartigen Aufbau fast russisch-orthodox und erinnern an Tschaikowskys Stück *In der Kirche* (*Kinderalbum Op. 39*). Das Stück stammt aus einer Werksammlung nach Hans Christian Andersons Märchen.

Johannes Brahms (1833–1897)
23. Walzer Op. 39 No. 5
Der Walzer stammt aus den Eigenarrangements des Komponisten seiner 16 Walzer. In seiner Bearbeitung fängt Brahms trotz des vereinfachten Aufbaus geschickt das Wesen der Stücke ein. In Takt 1-8 sollte das Crescendo in der Oberstimme hervorgehoben werden, während die beidhändigen Melodiestimmen in Takt 9 und 11 gleichwertig gespielt werden sollten. Brahms schrieb zahlreiche Arrangements zu verschiedenen Zwecken, u.a. als technische Herausforderungen (Webers *Perpetuum mobile*, in dem die schnellen Sechzehntel auf die linke Hand übertragen wurden), Geburtstagsgeschenke für Freunde (Variationen aus seinem eigenen *Streichsextett op. 18*, bearbeitet für Soloklavier) und als Übungen (kürzere Bach-Arrangements).

Johann Burgmüller (1806–1874)
1. Pastorale Op. 100 No. 3
Dieses kurze Stück ist ein hervorragendes Übungsstück zur unterschiedlichen Gewichtung der Melodietöne in der rechten und der Akkorde in der linken Hand. Die Akkorde sollten zwar mit Nachdruck gespielt werden, sich aber immer der Melodie unterordnen. Die Verwendung des Pedals gehört natürlich zu diesem Musikstil, obwohl die Noten keine Angaben enthalten. Ein eigenständiger Pedaleinsatz kann betonte Stellen im Stück, z.B. die ersten Schläge in Takt 11-14, bereichern.

25. Ballade Op. 100 No. 15
Diese *Ballade* ist nach wie vor bei Klavierlehrern und -schülern sehr beliebt. Sie ist leicht spielbar, wirkt in unterschiedlichen Grundtempi und ist für die Koordination der rechten und linken Hand ausgesprochen nützlich, vor allem in Takt 3-4. Im Mittelteil lernen die Schüler, die Melodietöne auf dem ersten Schlag im Takt zu spielen, während die linke Hand das rhythmische Gefüge beibehält. Die Takte 87-91 erfordern eine besonders gute Koordination. Um diese zu üben, sollten die Takte mit überkreuzten Händen gespielt werden – sowohl die rechte über die linke als auch umgekehrt. Wenn man die Takte anschließend wieder wie notiert spielt, merkt man, wie nützlich das Überkreuzspielen sein kann!

Frédéric Chopin (1810–1849)
14. Wiosna (Spring) BI 117
Dieses Arrangement vom 5. Februar 1846 ist eine von zwei Liedbearbeitungen, die Chopin von seinen eigenen Werken anfertigte; die andere befindet sich in Band 3 der *Romantic Piano Anthology* (ED 12914). Das Halten eines Grundtons, während die linke Hand etwas anderes spielt, ähnelt dem Prinzip von Tschaikowskys *Old French Song* (Nr. 15 in dieser Sammlung). Um beide Stimmen bequem zu spielen, kann man das tiefe G halten und gleichzeitig die Oberstimme in der linken Hand als langsame, abgestoßene Achtelfigur spielen. Wenn das klappt, kann man beide Stimmen wie notiert legato ausprobieren.

Diese selten gespielte Miniatur von Chopin erschien erstmals 1968 bei Schott. Herausgeber war Ates Orga, der auch die CD zu dieser Sammlung produzierte. Unter den Pianisten ist *Wiosna* in der Bearbeitung von Franz Liszt am bekanntesten, dessen Version in Band 4 der *Romantic Piano Anthology* (ED 12915) enthalten ist.

24. Gallop Marquis (KKp 1240a)
Dies ist eine weitere selten gespielte Miniatur von Chopin. Das Achtelmotiv am Anfang erinnert an die ‚militärische' *Polonaise Op. 40 No. 1*. Die größten Herausforderungen des Stücks sind die Sprünge in der linken Hand in Takt 13-19. Zum Üben sollte ein wesentlich langsameres Tempo gewählt werden. Alle einzelnen Achtel in Takt 13-19 werden zunächst eine Oktave tiefer als notiert gespielt. Wenn das klappt, wird die Passage wie notiert gespielt und das Tempo allmählich gesteigert.

29. Boureé BI 160b No. 2
Das Stück wurde erstmals 1968 von Schott zusammen mit *Wiosna* (s.o.) und der *Boureé No. 1* (ED 12912) veröffentlicht. Der Herausgeber der Ausgabe, Ates Orga, schlägt zu Recht vor, die letzte Achtel in Takt 16 der rechten Hand aus harmonischen Gründen durch ein Cis zu ersetzen.

Antonín Dvořák (1841–1904)

7. Album Leaf B158

Die Originalhandschrift des Stücks ist auf den 21.07.1888 datiert. Der Komponist macht am Anfang keine Dynamikangaben; stattdessen deutet die Spielanweisung ‚innig' auf die Stimmung des Stücks und somit auch auf die Dynamik hin, die wahrscheinlich ein wenig lauter als ‚piano' ist. Die Aufteilung des Arpeggios im letzten Takt der linken Hand ist lediglich ein Vorschlag des Herausgebers.

Zdenko Fibich (1850–1900)

11. Capriccio

Dieses kurze Paradestück enthält einige technische Herausforderungen. Erstens erfordern die aufsteigenden Tonleitern ein gut vorbereitetes und daher lautloses Überkreuzspielen. Zweitens müssen die Tonwiederholungen in Takt 28 und 29 gründlich vorbereitet werden; der angegebene Fingersatz ist in diesem Abschnitt sicherlich eine bewährte Lösung. Wie so oft in Fibichs Musik wird das Stück grundsätzlich leise gespielt, und die *forte*-Angaben sollten zwar deutlich umgesetzt, aber nur kurz artikuliert werden.

26. Piece Op. 47 No. 1

Diese Miniatur vom 11.06.1895 ist eine der *376 Moods, Impressions and Reminiscences* (1892–99), ein Klavierzyklus, der aus der Verliebtheit des Komponisten in eine Schülerin entstand. Die Herausforderung des Stücks ist, die sich wiederholenden Triolen innerhalb eines gewissen dynamischen Rahmens einheitlich zu spielen. Dies führt unweigerlich zum Ausprobieren verschiedener Klangeigenschaften und ist daher eine interessante Alternative zu Chopins *Prelude Op. 28 No. 4*.

César Franck (1822–1890)

5. A Christmas Carol from Anjou (Aus: l'Organiste [1889–90])

Das Stück hat zwei Grundtempi. Das Anfangstempo wird bis zu Takt 16 gehalten. Anschließend wird das Stück langsamer, bis das neue Tempo in Takt 21 erreicht ist. Der Moll/Dur-Kontrast der beiden Abschnitte ist somit sowohl durch die Tonalität als auch durch das Grundtempo geprägt. In Takt 16–20 muss die Stimmführung sowohl in der Melodie- als auch in der Bassstimme deutlich zu hören sein.

9. Les plaintes d'une poupée (Der Puppe Klagelied, 1865)

Der Titel dieses Stücks deutet zwar auf ein langsames Grundtempo hin, doch wirkt es durch die Wahl einer Durtonart eher nachdenklich als traurig. Die Begleitung muss in einem gleichmäßigen Legato gespielt und der Melodie untergeordnet werden. Die rechte Hand spielt zwar im Großteil des Stücks die Melodie, doch muss die linke Hand in Takt 37–44 in den Vordergrund treten. Die fehlenden Phrasierungszeichen sind ein interessantes Merkmal des Stücks und bieten dem Schüler und Lehrer die Gelegenheit, mit der Musik zu experimentieren und ihr eine individuelle Note zu verleihen.

Michail Glinka (1804–1857)

8. Mazurka (1852)

Schüler mit kleineren Händen müssen die Akkorde mit den größeren Intervallen wahrscheinlich als Arpeggio spielen. Dies gilt vor allem für die Dezimen in Takt 4 und 7 und eventuell auch für die Oktaven in Takt 7 und 15. Die *Mazurka* ist ein polnischer Volkstanz, der wahrscheinlich aus Mazovia, einer Region bei Warschau stammt. Der Tanz ist nicht zwangsläufig schnell, doch wird immer der zweite Taktschlag betont, ein Merkmal, das Glinka im ganzen Stück berücksichtigt (s. als Beispiel Takt 1 und 9). Die *Mazurka* war im 19. Jahrhundert ein beliebtes Instrumentalstück, vor allem durch Chopins Beiträge zu diesem Genre.

Charles Gounod (1818–1893)

12. Musette (1863)

Die *Musette* ist ein französischer Dudelsack mit vier bis fünf Borduntönen und war im 17. und 18. Jahrhundert sehr populär. Gounod imitiert diesen Bordun in den Quinten der linken Hand, über denen sich eine zunehmend fantasievolle Melodie entfaltet. In Takt 66 und 68ff sollte das erste H der Verzierung in der rechten Hand mit dem Akkord in der linken zusammenfallen. Die Takte 49-56 sind dreistimmig aufgebaut, wobei die punktierten Halben besonders betont werden müssen.

Enrique Granados (1867–1916)

4. *** Op. 1 No. 6

Granados' Stücke *Op. 1* erinnern sowohl in Bezug auf ihre Stimmung als auch auf die Harmonie ein wenig an Schumann. Schumanns Beispiel der Veröffentlichung eines Stück folgend, dessen Titel absichtlich nicht genannt wird (und der stattdessen mit *** gekennzeichnet ist), legt auch Granados hier ein ‚geheimnisvolles' Stück vor. Die größte Herausforderung des ausnehmend einfachen Stücks ist das durchgängige Legato, das sowohl durch die Finger als auch durch das Pedal-Legato entsteht.

20. Dedicatoria Op. 1 No. 1

Dedicatoria ist eine sehr gute Übung für die Anschlagsdynamik. Da sowohl Begleitung als auch Bassstimme potenziell stärker sind als die Melodie mit dem 4. und 5. Finger, muss man das Stück zunächst wahrscheinlich mit einer *forte* gespielten Melodie üben, um sie von dem *piano*-Anschlag im Bass und in der Begleitung abzuheben. Wenn das klappt, kann die Lautstärke entsprechend reduziert werden. In Takt 9 und 11 wird die Melodie auf dem zweiten Taktschlag offbeat gespielt. Um dies zu betonen, sollte das hohe G etwas kräftiger gespielt werden als die vorherigen Melodietöne.

Edvard Grieg (1843–1907)

10. Halling Op. deest

Das Tempo für diesen norwegischen Tanz hängt vom Tempo der Sechzehntel in Takt 17 ab. Zuerst sollte man ein Tempo finden, in dem man diesen Abschnitt problemlos spielen kann und es dann auf den Anfang des Stückes übertragen. Die kurzen Vorschläge in Takt 9–16 sollten am besten mit einem ganz leichten Anschlag geübt werden, damit sie den Melodiefluss nicht stören. Sowohl *Halling* als auch das nachfolgende *Lullaby* (s.u.) stammen aus einer Sammlung mit *6 nordischen Melodien*, die erstmals 1886 veröffentlicht wurde.

17. Bådnlåt (Lullaby) Op. deest

Dieses *Schlaflied* kann recht langsam gespielt werden, doch müssen die Pedalangaben eventuell geändert werden, damit das Stück auf dem heutigen Klavier nicht überladen klingt. Ein Pedalwechsel auf jeder Viertel verleiht dem Stück Klangfülle, ohne erdrückend zu klingen. Um das Überkreuzspielen in Takt 17 und 18 zu unterstreichen, kann man die Töne für die linke Hand lauter spielen als die für die rechte.

27. Alvedans (Elves' Dance) Op. 12 No. 4

Der *Elfentanz* ist das vierte Stück in Griegs *Lyrischen Stücken op. 12*. Es entstand zwischen 1864 und 1867 und ist technisch und musikalisch sehr reizvoll zum Üben und Spielen. Die rechte Hand spielt die Melodie bis zum Auftakt in Takt 7, wo die linke Hand kurz die Melodie übernimmt. Die nächste Herausforderung ist der veränderte Aufbau sowie der Wechsel vom Violin- zum Bassschlüssel in Takt 16–17. Der erste Akkord von Takt 17 sollte so gut auf dem Schlag gespielt werden, wie es die schnellen Bewegungen der Hände gestatten. In Takt 23–30 ist eine Drehbewegung der rechten Hand erforderlich, damit sie sich nicht verkrampft, und um die angedeutete, mit Finger 1–3 gespielte Melodiestimme hervorzuheben. In den letzten drei Takten des Stücks gibt der Komponist eine Staccato-Anweisung für die Akkorde und gleichzeitig die Anweisung, durchgängig das Pedal zu treten. Dies kann als Anweisung für mehr Klangfülle verstanden werden, zu der die Staccato-Akkorde beitragen. Für die Aufnahme habe ich den Pedaleinsatz geändert und spiele die Staccato-Akkorde so kurz wie möglich.

Félix Le Couppey (1811–1887)
18. Étude Op. 22 No. 22

Dieses Stück stammt aus der Sammlung *24 Études primarie*, die erstmals von Schott veröffentlicht wurde. Zwei weitere Etüden sind bereits in Band 1 der *Romantic Piano Anthology* (ED 12912) enthalten. Die Metronomangaben stammen vom Komponisten. Rhythmisch besteht die Gefahr, die Pause zu kürzen. Daher ist es nützlich, den 6/8-Takt zunächst mit einem Akkord auf jedem Schlag zu spielen, bevor man den Rhythmus wie notiert übt.

Franz Liszt (1811–1886)
19. Walzer (1823)

Dieser Walzer klingt eher nach Schubert als nach Liszt. Er entstand 1823, als der Komponist erst zwölf war, und enthält keines der harmonischen Merkmale seiner späteren Stücke. Liszts ausführliche Artikulationsangaben in Takt 5 und 7 heben z. B. den Tanzcharakter des Stücks hervor und

sind daher wichtig für das stilistische Verständnis und die Suche nach einem geeigneten Tempo für diese Miniatur. Der Walzer ist ein Tanz im 3/4-Takt, der sich wahrscheinlich aus dem etwas langsameren österreichischen *Ländler* entwickelte.

22. Piano Piece No. 4 (1876)

Dieses Stück ist ein gutes Beispiel für den Stil, den der Komponist ab 1875 entwickelte. Es stammt aus einem Satz mit vier Stücken, die über mehrere Jahre entstanden und ist technisch nicht so komplex wie viele seiner früheren Stücke. Der Stil erfordert einen durchgängigen Einsatz des Pedals, obwohl nur die Takte 14–15 und 20–21 entsprechende Angaben enthalten. Eine gute Alternative zu Liszts Pedaleinsatz in Takt 15 wäre ein sehr schneller Pedaleinsatz auf jeder Achtel, die dann einen dezenten Nachklang aus dem vorherigen Akkord enthält. Dies führt zu einem leicht verschwommenen Klang, der aber noch im Einklang mit der ursprünglichen Intention des Komponisten ist. Das Arpeggio der letzten zwei Takte sollte großzügig gespielt werden, um Zeit für das *più ritenuto* bis zum Schluss zu haben.

Sergej Ljapunow (1859–1924)
13. Berceuse d'une poupée (Schlaflied einer Puppe, 1914)

Der Rhythmus ist zwar für jede Hand einzeln ganz einfach, doch kann es beim beidhändigen Spiel zu Koordinationsproblemen kommen. Es kann hilfreich sein, die Takte 3–10 in Einheiten aus zweieinhalb Takten in verschiedenen Tempi zu spielen (eine Phrase besteht aus 2 Takten; ein halber Takt sollte als Verbindung zur nächsten Phrase einkalkuliert werden). Wenn in Takt 21 eine weitere Stimme für die rechte Hand hinzukommt, wird die Koordination beider Hände merkwürdigerweise oft leichter!

Hugo Reinhold (1854–1935)
30. Hungarian Dance Op. 19 No. 13

Reinholds Stück ist sehr einprägsam und verfügt über das wesentliche Element einiger Vorzeigestücke: Es klingt schwieriger, als es ist. Der Rhythmus sollte außer im *ritardando*-Abschnitt in der Mitte des Stücks streng eingehalten werden. Die schwierigsten Takte sind wahrscheinlich Takt 5–8 und 26–29. Beide Hände müssen exakt zusammenspielen, wobei sich die rechte Hand der linken anpassen muss und nicht umgekehrt. So lässt sich das Zusammenspiel leichter kontrollieren und gestalten.

Franz Schubert (1797–1828)
2. Walzer D365 No. 28

Schuberts *Walzer* stammt aus einer Walzersammlung, die zwischen 1816 und 1821 entstand. Das Stück wirkt in unterschiedlichen Tempi gleich gut. Je nachdem, ob man es eher als Walzer oder als Ländler betrachtet, kann es entweder lebhaft oder mäßig schnell gespielt werden. In beiden Fällen besteht die größte Herausforderung im gleichmäßigen Klang des Pralltrillers. Die Verzierung sollte als Achteltriole geübt werden, die zum nächsten Schlag führt. Dadurch hat man Zeit, um einen klaren, gleichmäßigen Klang zu erzeugen.

Robert Schumann (1810–1856)
3. Wilder Reiter Op. 68 No. 8
Der *Wilder Reiter* ist sowohl zum Üben als auch zum Vorspielen gut geeignet, da hier einige Techniken geübt werden, das Stück aber auch ein wirkungsvolles und schönes Vortragsstück ist. Der technische Vorteil der Staccato-Achtelfiguren ist, dass sie in der jeweiligen Tonart klar erkennbar für eine Hand notiert sind. Die gebundenen Legato-Noten bieten eine hilfreiche Pause, bevor es zum nächsten Satz Staccato-Noten geht. Letztendlich ist es jedoch die abwechslungsreiche Melodie, die das Stück bei Lehrern und Schülern gleichermaßen beliebt macht.

16. Sizilianisch Op. 68 No. 11
Dieses Stück hat etwas Spielerisches und Stichelndes. Im 6/8-Abschnitt kommen die beiden Eigenschaften durch den Wechsel zwischen *piano* und *forte* gut zur Geltung. Beim Erlernen des Stücks erfordert jedoch der 2/4-Abschnitt mehr Zeit, vor allem die linke Hand in Takt 28 und 29. Um den 5. Finger auf dem Fis zu platzieren, muss man eventuell den 3. Finger weiter unten als gewohnt auf das ‚a' legen. Trotzdem ist dies wahrscheinlich die bequemste Möglichkeit für diese Passage.

Peter Iljitsch Tschaikowsky (1840–1893)
15. Old French Song (Altfranzösisches Lied) Op. 39 No. 16
Das *Altfranzösische Lied* zeichnet sich nicht nur durch eine abwechslungsreiche Melodie aus, sondern ist auch gut zur Weiterentwicklung der Unabhängigkeit der Finger der linken Hand geeignet. Vom musikalischen Standpunkt aus sollte ein Tempo gewählt werden, in dem man sich ein Streichinstrument vorstellen kann, das alle Melodietöne spielt und miteinander verbindet. In Takt 18–20 sollten die Noten für die linke Hand so abgestoßen wie möglich gespielt werden, ohne den Fluss und die Dominanz der Melodie in der rechten Hand zu stören. Auch hier enthalten die Noten keine Pedalanweisungen. Das Pedal ist ein fester Bestandteil des Stils.

28. Sweet Dream (Süßer Traum) Op. 39 No. 21
Der Einsatz des Pedals in diesem Stück folgt der Melodie und somit der grundlegenden Harmoniefolge der Musik. Die dynamischen Kontraste sind wichtig, vor allem die *forte*-Klänge, die vor allem beim ersten Spielen etwas hart klingen können. Die gegensätzlichen Gefühle des Stücks kommen jedoch nur zur Geltung, wenn der dynamische Kontrast stimmt. An einigen Stellen mit Kadenzen, z. B. Takt 8–9, 16–17 etc., ist es ganz normal, dass man sich etwas Zeit lässt, bis das Grundtempo wieder erreicht ist. In Takt 21–24 und 29–32 sollten die Offbeat-Akkorde so leicht gespielt werden, dass der Melodiefluss der Viertel nicht unterbrochen wird.

Biografische Anmerkungen

Sergej Bortkiewicz (1877–1952)
Der Ukrainer Sergej Bortkiewicz verbrachte den Großteil seines Lebens als Pianist und Klavierlehrer in Österreich und Deutschland. Er studierte von 1896 bis 1899 bei Ljadow am Sankt Petersburger Konservatorium und setzte sein Klavier- und Kompositionsstudium bei Reisenauer und Jadassohn am Leipziger Konservatorium fort. Musikalisch ist Bortkiewicz' Stil von Chopin, Liszt und dem frühen Rachmaninow beeinflusst. Er blieb sein ganzes Leben lang der tonalen Kompositionsform treu, die ihre Wurzeln im Russland des späten 19. Jahrhunderts hat.

Johannes Brahms (1833–1897)
Brahms wurde zwar in Hamburg geboren, verbrachte aber den Großteil seines Lebens in Wien, wo er ab 1862 einer der einflussreichsten Komponisten des 19. Jahrhunderts wurde. Er wurde 1853 durch Robert Schumanns begeisterte Rezension berühmt, in der er ihn als ‚Berufenen' bezeichnete. Brahms entwickelte eine sehr individuelle Klaviernotation, die von mehrstimmigen Akkorden, Doppeltönen und Polyrhythmik geprägt war. Sein kompositorischer Einfluss ist in der gesamten zweiten Hälfte des 19. sowie am Anfang des 20. Jahrhunderts spürbar, u.a. auf Reger und Stanford.

Johann Burgmüller (1806–1874)
Johann Burgmüller wurde in Regensburg geboren und ging 1832 nach Paris, wo er als begehrter Klavierlehrer und Komponist von Übungsstücken lebte. Seine Etüden *op. 73, 100* und *105* sind längst fester Bestandteil des Klavierrepertoires für Schüler. Burgmüller schrieb in einem zugänglichen Stil mit einprägsamen, auf das Klavier zugeschnittenen Melodien.

Frédéric Chopin (1810–1849)
Der gebürtige Pole übersiedelte 1831 nach Frankreich, wo er als Komponist und privater Klavierlehrer arbeitete. Chopin trat nur selten öffentlich auf und erwarb sich seinen Ruf durch ausgewählte Konzertauftritte und die Veröffentlichung seiner Werke. Er bediente sich zwar oft ‚populärer' Genres wie *Walzer*, *Präludien* und *Etüden*, doch war sein Stil ebenso unverkennbar wie zeitlos. Chopin etablierte die *Ballade* als instrumentales Klavierstück, machte die *Mazurka* im 19. Jahrhundert populär und entwickelte nach John Field das Genre der *Nocturne* weiter. Sein bedeutendster Beitrag zur Entwicklung der Klaviertechnik waren seine *Etüden Op. 10* und *Op. 25*.

Antonín Dvořák (1841–1904)
Dvořák war einer der wenigen bedeutenden Komponisten des 19. Jahrhunderts, deren erstes Instrument nicht das Klavier war. Er studierte Violine und wurde anschließend Berufsbratschist, bevor seine Karriere als Komponist begann. Dvořák wurde von der traditionellen tschechischen

Volksmusik und seinem engen freundschaftlichen Kontakt zu Brahms beeinflusst. Als Kompositionslehrer unterrichtete er die nächste Generation junger tschechischer Komponisten, u.a. Suk und Novák.

Zdenko Fibich (1850–1900)

Der tschechische Komponist Zdenko Fibich studierte von 1865 bis 1867 am Leipziger Konservatorium. Zu seinen Lehrern zählten Moscheles (Klavier), Richter und Jadassohn (Komposition). Fibich lebte kurz in Paris und Mannheim, bevor er sich in Prag niederließ. Hier arbeitete er als Theaterdirigent und Komponist. Seine breit gefächerten Werke beinhalten Sinfonien, Lieder, Kammermusik, Opern sowie eine Sammlung aus Klavierstücken mit dem Titel *376 Moods, Impressions and Reminiscences* (aus der die beiden Stücke dieser Anthologie stammen). Viele dieser Miniaturen zeigen seine Vorliebe für leise Stücke und nachdenkliche Stimmungen.

César Franck (1822–1890)

César Franck hatte eine bedeutende musikalische Karriere als Künstler, bevor er die Werke schrieb, die ihm seine Stellung als einer der größten Komponisten seiner Zeit sicherten. Er wurde 1822 in Belgien geboren und ging mit 13 Jahren nach Paris, um am Konservatorium Komposition zu studieren. Nach seinem Abschluss 1842 wurde er Chorleiter und Organist. Franck war für sein Improvisationstalent bekannt und komponierte weiterhin, obwohl ihm erst die Werke, die er ab Ende der 1870er-Jahre schrieb, dauerhafte internationale Anerkennung als Komponist einbrachten.

Michail Glinka (1804–1857)

Michail Glinka wird oft als ‚Vater der russischen Musik' bezeichnet. Er war wahrscheinlich der erste russische Komponist, dessen Werke außerhalb Russlands bekannt wurden. Glinka lebte eine Zeit lang in Mailand, Wien und Berlin, bevor er nach Russland zurückkehrte. Mit seiner Oper *Ein Leben für den Zaren* (1836) etablierte er sich als führender russischer Komponist seiner Zeit. Glinkas Musik beeinflusste zahlreiche jüngere russische Komponisten, vor allem Balakirew, Rimski-Korsakow und Mussorgski.

Charles Gounod (1818–1893)

Der französische Komponist, Organist und Dirigent schrieb Opern, Instrumentalmusik, Kantaten und Kirchenmusik. Gounod komponierte nur wenige Klavierstücke, die jedoch die für ihn charakteristischen melodischen und harmonischen Stilmerkmale aufweisen. Sein erster Erfolg war vielleicht auch sein größter und dauerhaftester: die Oper *Faust* von 1859.

Enrique Granados (1867–1916)

Dem spanischen Komponisten und Pianisten Enrique Granados gelang die mühelose Verschmelzung eines zugänglichen Klavierstils mit unverkennbar spanischen Musikstücken. Als engagierter Lehrer gründete er eine eigene Musikschule, die Academia Granados, die nach dem Tod des Komponisten unter der Leitung seines ehemaligen Schülers Frank Marshall fortgeführt wurde. Granados schrieb zahlreiche Werke für Klavier, von Fingerübungen, Etüden und kurzen Charakterstücken bis hin zu Konzertrepertoirestücken.

Edvard Grieg (1843–1907)

Der norwegische Komponist, Lehrer und Pianist studierte nach seiner ersten Ausbildung in seiner Heimat am Leipziger Konservatorium. Seine Musik fand schon bald bei seinen Zeitgenossen Beachtung, vor allem bei Liszt, der 1870 angeblich Griegs Klavierkonzert vom Blatt spielte und den Komponisten bestärkte. Als Komponist schrieb Grieg angeblich bevorzugt kürzere Stücke. Sein bekanntestes Klavierwerk, eine Sammlung aus zehn Alben mit dem Titel *Lyrische Stücke*, nimmt nach wie vor einen wichtigen Platz im Klavierrepertoire ein.

Félix le Couppey (1811–1887)

Le Couppey war Professor für Klavier am Pariser Konservatorium und wurde 1843 als Professor für Harmonielehre Nachfolger seines eigenen Lehrers. 1847 vertrat er den Klaviervirtuosen Henri Herz und bekam anschließend eine eigene Klavierklasse. Heute ist le Couppey für seine einflussreichen pädagogischen Werke bekannt, u.a. *L'ABC du Piano* und *24 Études primaires*. Er schrieb zahlreiche Stücke für Anfänger, die seine melodische Begabung widerspiegeln. Das vorliegende Stück stammt aus der Sammlung *24 Études primaires*, die erstmals von Schott veröffentlicht wurde.

Franz Liszt (1811–1886)

Liszt war einer der einflussreichsten, umstrittensten und schillerndsten Pianisten und Komponisten des 19. Jahrhunderts. Als Schüler des Beethoven-Schülers Czerny war Liszt ein Wunderkind, das mit 17 Jahren zu den führenden Pianisten seiner Zeit gehörte. Nachdem er Anfang der 1830er-Jahre Paganini in Paris gehört hatte, beschloss Liszt, sich selbst soweit fortzubilden, dass er als Pianist genauso gut wurde wie Paganini als Geiger. Dementsprechend schrieb Liszt sehr anspruchsvolle Werke, was ihm den Ruf eines brillanten Virtuosen eintrug. 1848 zog sich Liszt von seinen Konzertreisen als Pianist zurück, um sich aufs Dirigieren und Komponieren zu konzentrieren. Er förderte viele junge Pianisten und erweiterte durch seine Kompositionen die Grenzen der Harmonik und Tonalität.

Sergej Ljapunow (1859–1924)

Sergej Ljapunow war ein russischer Komponist, Pianist und Dirigent. Seine Entwicklung als Komponist wurde vom russischen Nationalismus Balakirews, von der östlichen Volksmusik und von Liszts Klavierspiel beeinflusst. Diese Merkmale verschmolzen zu einem sehr individuellen, eleganten und virtuosen Kompositionsstil. Das vorliegende Stück stammt aus der Sammlung *Sechs leichte Stücke*, die 1914 entstand.

Hugo Reinhold (1854–1935)

Der gebürtige Wiener Hugo Reinhold war bis 1874 Chormitglied der Hofkapelle. Anschließend studierte er am Wiener Konservatorium bei Bruckner Komposition und arbeitete ab 1897 auch dort. Von 1909 bis 1925 unterrichtete Reinhold an der Universität für Musik und darstellende Kunst in Wien. Sein Werk enthält mehrere Sammlungen für Klavierschüler, u.a. das *Jugendalbum Op. 27*, *Kleine melodische Etüden Op. 56* sowie *Jugenderinnerungen Op. 5*. Die meisten dieser Stücke sind leicht zugänglich und sehr melodisch.

Franz Schubert (1797–1828)

Im Gegensatz zu vielen seiner Zeitgenossen war Schubert weder ein virtuoser Künstler noch ein zu Lebzeiten berühmter Komponist. Schubert, der eigentlich Grundschullehrer werden wollte, widmete sich ab 1817 vollständig dem Komponieren. Er schuf zahlreiche hervorragende Werke, darunter 600 Lieder, Kammermusik, neun Sinfonien und viele Klavierwerke. Ein Großteil der Musik wurde zu Lebzeiten Schuberts nicht aufgeführt oder veröffentlicht. Schuberts Stil ist von einem bis heute unerreichten melodischen Einfallsreichtum geprägt.

Robert Schumann (1810–1856)

Robert Schumann war einer der einflussreichsten Komponisten des 19. Jahrhunderts. Er entwickelte eine eigene musikalische Sprache, die von zwei gegensätzlichen Fantasiefiguren geprägt wurde: Florestan und Eusebius. Sie repräsentierten das extravagante und ausdrucksvolle Wesen seiner Musik (und seines Charakters). Schumann bediente sich vieler literarischer Vorlagen, vor allem der Romane von E.T.A. Hoffmann, und seine Musik ist häufig die direkte Umsetzung einer literarischen Quelle. Bis 1839 schrieb Schumann fast ausschließlich Klaviermusik, bevor er sich auch Kammermusik, Liedern und Orchesterwerken widmete. Stilistische übte er auf zahlreiche Komponisten des 19. Jahrhunderts, von Kirchner bis Tschaikowsky, einen spürbaren Einfluss aus.

Peter Iljitsch Tschaikowsky (1840–1893)

Der russische Komponist und Dirigent Peter Iljitsch Tschaikowsky studierte zuerst Jura und arbeitete als Beamter, bevor er sich voll und ganz dem Komponieren widmete. Tschaikowsky erlangte in den 1880er- und 1890er-Jahren internationale Anerkennung. Ein Großteil seiner Orchester- und Ballettmusik zeichnet sich durch abwechslungsreiche Melodien und eine reichhaltige Instrumentierung aus. Tschaikowskys Klavierwerke reichen vom umfangreichen Konzertrepertoire wie die *Große Sonate G-Dur Op. 37* bis zum *Kinderalbum Op. 39* für junge Pianisten.

Further Piano Titles available from Schott

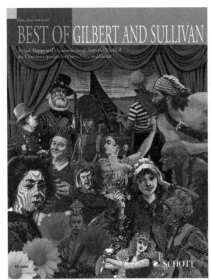

Improvising Blues Piano
Tim Richards
ED 12504

Exploring Jazz Piano
Tim Richards
ED 12708 (Vol. 1)
ED 12829 (Vol. 2)

'Best of' Series
Arranged by Barrie Carson Turner
Best of Folk Songs ED 12880
Best of Christmas Carols ED 12766
Best of Children's Songs ED 12948

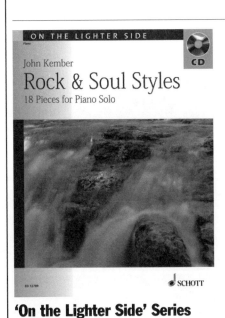

'On the Lighter Side' Series
John Kember
Rock & Soul Styles
ED 12789
16 Pieces for Piano Solo
ED 12614
9 Pieces for Piano Duet
ED 12615
Blues Pieces for Piano Solo
ED 12726

10 Christmas Carols for Piano Duet
ED 12645
12 Spirituals for Piano Solo and Duet
arranged by John Kember ED 12659
Latin Pieces for Piano Duet
ED 12695
On the Lighter Side Collection (Solos)
ED 12841
On the Lighter Side Collection (Duets)
ED 12842

Christmas titles
by Bill Readdy
We Wish You a Jazzy Christmas
ED 12668
Christmas Jive will Holly and Ive
ED 12727
Twinkle, Twinkle Jazzy Star
ED 12728

Send for a copy of the Schott Piano Music Catalogue
Website: www.schott-music.com

Mainz · London · Madrid · New York · Paris · Prague · Tokyo · Toronto

CD Track List / Plages du CD / CD-Titelverzeichnis

No.	Title	Composer	Duration
1	Pastorale Op. 100 No. 3	Johann Burgmüller	01:00
2	Waltzer D365 No. 28	Franz Schubert	00:36
3	Wilder Reiter Op. 68 No. 8	Robert Schumann	00:39
4	* * * Op. 1 No. 6	Enrique Granados	00:45
5	A Christmas Carol from Anjou	César Franck	00:53
6	Venedig: Gondellied	Sergey Bortkiewicz	01:59
7	Album Leaf B158 Op. 21 No. 10	Antonín Dvořák	00:53
8	Mazurka (1852)	Mikhail Glinka	00:45
9	Les plaintes d'une poupée (1865)	César Franck	01:22
10	Halling Op. deest	Edvard Grieg	00:34
11	Capriccio Op. deest	Zdenko Fibich	01:02
12	Musette (1863)	Charles Gounod	01:40
13	Berceuse d'une poupée (1914)	Sergey Lyapounov	01:52
14	Wiosna BI. 117	Frédéric Chopin	00:58
15	Old French Song Op. 39 No. 16	Peter Ilyich Tchaikovsky	00:55
16	Sizilianisch Op. 68 No. 11	Robert Schumann	01:31
17	Bådnlåt Op. deest	Edvard Grieg	01:12
18	Étude Op. 22 No. 22	Félix Le Couppey	01:11
19	Waltzer (1823)	Franz Liszt	00:44
20	Dedicatoria Op. 1 No. 1	Enrique Granados	00:54
21	Der Engel Op. 30 No. 4	Sergey Bortkiewicz	01:47
22	Piano Piece No. 4 (1876)	Franz Liszt	00:59
23	Waltzer Op. 39 No. 5	Johannes Brahms	01:16
24	Gallop Marquis KKp 1240a	Frédéric Chopin	00:59
25	Ballade Op. 100 No. 15	Johann Burgmüller	01:24
26	Piece Op. 47 No. 1	Zdenko Fibich	01:24
27	Alvedans Op. 12 No. 4	Edvard Grieg	01:02
28	Sweet Dream Op. 39 No. 21	Peter Ilyich Tchaikovsky	01:47
29	Bourée BI. 160b No. 2	Frédéric Chopin	00:36
30	Hungarian Dance Op. 39 No. 13	Hugo Reinhold	00:55

Total duration 33:37